THE FACILITATORS' HANDBOOK

THE
FACILITATORS'
HANDBOOK

John Heron

Kogan Page, London/Nichols Publishing, New York

First published in Great Britain in 1989 by
Kogan Page Ltd, 120 Pentonville Road, London N1 9JN

Printed and bound in Great Britain by
Biddles Ltd, Guildford

British Library Cataloguing in Publication Data
Heron, John
    The facilitators' handbook
    1. Great Britain. Personnel. Training. Method: Group
    discussions. Leadership
    I. Title
658.3' 12404

    ISBN .i.0-7494-0010-2

First published in the United States of America in 1989 by
Nichols Publishing, an imprint of GP Publishing Inc.,
PO Box 96, New York, NY 10024

Library of Congress Cataloging-in-Publication Data
Heron, John, 1928-
    The facilitators' handbook/John Heron.
    p. cm.
    Includes bibliographical references.
    ISBN 0-89397-355-6: $26.50
    1. Group relations training. 2. Experiential learning.
    I. Title.
    HM134.H46   1989
    302' .14--dc20   89-23114
                    CIP

Contents

Foreword

The first edition of this book was published as *Dimensions of Facilitator Style* in 1977. The seeds of it were sown when I was a boy at the University of Toronto Schools in Toronto, Canada, comparing the different styles of the Canadian teachers and the English teachers I had known previously. Decades later, in 1974, issues of style arose again in discussions with Tom and Dency Sargent of Change Agents in Hartford, Connecticut, as we initiated the founding of Co-counselling International. By then, the issues were cast in their contemporary form relating to facilitator style. The central one was the reconciliation of the learner's autonomy with the facilitator's authority.

The American debate on this theme has been vital, from Kurt Lewin's inauguration of action research in the late 1940s and Carl Rogers' seminal 1969 book *Freedom to Learn*, to the influential work of William Knowles on self-directed learning and of William Torbert on liberating structures and collaborative inquiry.

The second edition of this book continues to address the same central theme. However, I have not simply edited the original text, but completely rewritten it, with fundamental conceptual development of the earlier model.

This revision has had three other main sources in the intervening years. The first has been my own development in facilitating experiential learning groups of diverse kinds. The second has been the continued use of the model, by myself and my colleagues, to train facilitators from many settings, through professional development programmes in the Department of Educational Studies at the University of Surrey and, up to 1985, in the British Postgraduate Medical Federation of the University of London. The third source has been the Institute for the Development of Human Potential, founded in London in 1977 by a group of facilitators, of which I was one, who wished to inaugurate two-year courses in humanistic psychology, based on experiential learning in groups and learner participation in educational decision-making. With courses running concurrently at five different centres, the Institute, through its committee of past and present course facilitators, has been a powerful crucible for inquiry into facilitation issues.

Thus the framework of ideas presented here has been forged at the workface of training. It has been created to do justice to the immediate reality of group work, and the claims it makes on the group leader. Although it is an original construct, it overlaps in several areas with many other theories and approaches in the field, whose influence over the years I have assimilated into my thinking and to the authors of which I acknowledge a special debt of gratitude. I have not wanted to labour the text with comparisons and contrasts: knowledgeable readers will be able to do that for themselves.

The key to facilitation, in the learning revolution that is currently afoot, is great flexibility of style in making educational decisions. The effective facilitator, who wants to provide conditions for the development of autonomous learning, is one who can move swiftly and elegantly, as the context requires, between three political modes: making decisions for learners, making decisions with learners, and delegating decisions to learners.

The effective facilitator is also one who can bring this flexibility to bear upon six main dimensions of the learning group: course planning, issues of meaning, confronting resistances, issues of feeling, structuring the immediate learning experience, valuing personhood.

The model of facilitation in this book applies the three modes to each of the six dimensions to offer 18 forms of facilitation. A range of specific interventions is given under each of these 18 forms. The result is a wide-ranging repertoire of options, which each person can use to fashion their unique facilitator style.

This work is offered as a reference manual for experienced facilitators who want to enhance their style; and as a resource book for training initial and in-service facilitators. It has to be used imaginatively and, above all, selectively.

Rooted in experience, the model presented here is provisional only. It is for future facilitators, in co-operation both with each other and with their learning groups, to enrich and revise it through further experience and reflection. This is in the spirit of co-operative inquiry, a new research paradigm that commends doing research *with* people, rather than doing research *on* them (Reason, 1988).

I am grateful to the large number of participants in my trainers' workshops, whose intelligent and caring commitment to their work has contributed so much to my thinking about facilitator style; to my present and past colleagues in the three institutions mentioned above for the stimulus of their creative thinking; to John Mulligan, Director of the Human Potential Resource Group, University of Surrey, for proposing and encouraging this work, and for many valuable comments on the first draft, which contributed greatly to the final version; and to Peter Reason for a helpful review of the second draft, and for much innovative collaboration over the years in the field of co-operative inquiry.

John Heron
London, June, 1989

1. Dimensions and modes

Background

This book is a complete rewrite of an earlier one with the title *Dimensions of Facilitator Style* (Heron, 1977). The first one was, before publication, revised after being field-tested in several training workshops on styles of group facilitation. As a result, it has been in continuous use for 12 years, at the University of Surrey and elsewhere, as a basis for training the trainers' workshops. However, this long application has thrown into relief the need for some extensive and significant changes. While the six dimensions remain basically the same, they have been remodelled to make the total system more coherent and comprehensive. Each dimension is given a single name title, instead of the old double-barrelled one. All but two of the original names are changed, to give them more breadth. In particular, the old cathartic dimension has been widened to become the feeling dimension.

The simple polarity - of directive/nondirective, etc. - has been enlarged. What was lurking within it has been made fully explicit. Each dimension is now seen as falling under the three political modes of hierarchy, co-operation and autonomy. This is the most important revision, and gives much more clarity and power to the whole analysis of facilitator options. And it has made it possible to include more interventions under the different dimensions, and to order them in a more coherent way.

There are two other major changes. The short passage on group dynamics in the first book has been greatly expanded here into a much more comprehensive theory. The long section on research, training and other issues has been greatly reduced.

The facilitator and the experiential group

What I mean by a *facilitator* in this book is a person who has the role of helping participants to learn in an experiential group. The facilitator will normally be formally appointed to this role by whatever organization is sponsoring the group. And the group members will voluntarily accept the facilitator in this role.

By an *experiential group* I mean one in which learning takes place through an active and aware involvement of the whole person - as a spiritual, thinking, feeling, choosing, energetically and physically embodied being. This covers a wide spectrum: traditional therapy groups, sensitivity training groups, encounter groups, personal growth groups in a particular mode (such as psychodrama, co-counselling, bio-energetics, primal, Gestalt, transpersonal, etc.), interpersonal skills training groups for personal or professional development, management training groups, social action training groups, etc.

The main focus throughout the text is on personal development and interactive skills groups, of the various kinds just mentioned. This is because the most searching issues for the facilitator come up in these contexts. However, I must stress that the model applies equally to groups which, learning through action and practice, are dealing with more external and technical skills, such as nursing and medical skills, and many others. I leave it to the imagination of the reader to adapt the text, and the selection of interventions, to these highly important contexts of learning.

The modern revolution in learning

There has been a radical change in the theory and practice of higher and continuing education over recent decades (Boud, 1988; Knowles, 1980). This is most evident in the fields of adult and continuing professional education. The basic and very simple premise of this change is that student learning is necessarily self-directed: it rests on the autonomous exercise of intelligence, choice and interest. From this many other points unfold, which I express here in terms of my own thinking about the basic issues involved:

1. Facilitation of learning. Teaching is no longer seen as imparting and doing things to the student, but is redefined as *facilitation of self-directed learning*. How people learn, and how to bring about this process, become the focus of concern, rather than the old-style pre-occupation with how to teach things to people; and with this goes a significant shift in the onus of responsibility. In the old model, the teacher is principally responsible for student learning. In the new model, the primary responsibility rests with the self-directing learner; and only secondarily with the facilitator.

2. Manifold learning. Learning itself I see as having four interdependent forms, which in many different ways complement and support each other.

Practical learning. This is learning how to do something. It involves the acquisition of a skill and it is expressed in the competent practice of that skill. This is the will, including the physical, level of learning.

Conceptual learning. This is learning about some subject matter, learning that something is the case; and is expressed in statements and propositions. This is the intellectual, verbal-conceptual level of learning.

Imaginal learning. This is learning configurations of form and process. It involves an intuitive grasp of a whole, as shape or sequence. It is expressed in the symbolism of line, shape, colour, proportion, succession, sound, rhythm, movement. This is the intuitive, image level of learning.

Experiential learning. This kind of learning is by encounter, by direct acquaintance, by entering *into* some state of being. It is manifest through the process of being there, face-to-face, with the person, at the event, in the experience. This is the feeling, resonance level of learning.

These four forms of learning are distinct; they cannot be reduced to each other. At the same time, however, they inform, support and enhance each other. They constitute an up-hierarchy, with the ones higher in this list being grounded in those that are lower, as shown in figure 1.1.

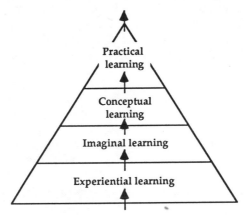

Figure 1.1 *Manifold learning*

We encounter the world (experiential learning); identify patterns of form and process in it (imaginal learning); these become the basis for the development of language and knowledge (conceptual learning) which is applied in a wide range of skills (practical learning). Henceforth, I use 'experiential learning' to refer to the whole hierarchy. This hierarchy states what kind of learning rests epistemologically on what other kind. But a formal learning cycle can take different routes through the four.

3. Holism in course design. The learner is a whole person, and the whole person needs to be involved in learning. Learning is extended from its traditional restriction to the theoretical and applied intellect, into the domains of body awareness, feelings and attitudes, interpersonal relations, social and political processes, psychic and spiritual awareness. This means three things.

Confluent education. The holistic, multi-stranded curriculum which attends - with differing degress of emphasis (depending on the primary learning objectives) - to body, emotions, intellect, will, psychic and spiritual dimensions of the person.

Task-process integration. The interweaving of a concern for human process with a commitment to the external tasks of learning about the world and how to apply knowledge to it.

Experiential learning cycle. This cycle either grounds thought in practice and encounter; or generates thought out of practice and encounter. So there are two complementary versions of the cycle. The first starts with a concept, cashes it out in appropriate experience, then reviews the concept in the light of so grounding it. The second starts with a certain kind of experience, distils a conceptual model out of this, then takes the model back into experience to develop and refine it.

4. Participation with staff. The concept of learning as self-directed only appeared in the old approach as students working on their own on prescribed tasks. The new approach applies it to participating with staff in three main areas of educational decision-making. To educate persons means to facilitate their self-direction not only in learning *what* the content of a discipline is, but also in learning *how* to learn it, and in learning *whether* they have learnt it. Hence the importance of the following two kinds of participation.

The learning contract. The student, at the appropriate stage, is invited to co-operate with staff in decisions about learning objectives, timetabling, pacing, teaching and learning methods, and the use of human and physical resources. Such collaborative course design may involve both one-to-one contracts and one-to-group contracts between facilitator and learners.

Collaborative assessment. The student takes part with the facilitator in determining criteria for assessment; each assesses the student's work in the light of these criteria, and together they negotiate the final grade. I have written about this in some detail elsewhere (Heron, 1988).

5. Co-operation with peers. Persons can only be self-directing in reciprocal relations with other self-directing persons. The autonomy of the learner entails a context of co-operation with other learners. Hence the importance of group-based learning, of student interdependence with regard to both experience and reflection, of peer problem-solving and decision-making, of peer feedback on practice, of self- and peer assessment. The autonomous learning group is an essential context for the new educational approach.

These five points taken together constitute the educational rationale for this book, and its account of facilitator options. It is committed to the view that the facilitator is a midwife eliciting the emergence of self-directed and peer learning.

The parameters of experiential learning

The participants are learning from experience. There are the *objectives of learning*: the knowledge, skills, and changes of attitude, affect and character structure to be acquired by the learners.

These, in turn, determine the *programme of learning*, that is, the curriculum, the course or workshop design which distributes different sorts of activity over a timetable.

This design includes the *methods of learning*: the different ways in which the participants acquire their knowledge and skills.

There are the *dimensions of facilitation*: different basic issues in relation to which the facilitator can influence the learning process.

Then come the *modes of facilitation*: the different ways in which the facilitator can handle decision-making within each dimension.

Here I summarize the *dimensions* and the *modes*.

The six dimensions of facilitation

1. The planning dimension. This is the goal-oriented, end-and-means, aspect of facilitation: that is, it is to do with the aims of the group, and what programme it should undertake to fulfil them. The facilitative question here is: how shall the group acquire its objectives and its programme?

2. The meaning dimension. This is the cognitive aspect of facilitation: it is to do with participants' understanding of what is going on, with their making sense of experience, and with their knowing how to do things and to react to things. The facilitative question is: how shall meaning be given to and found in the experiences and actions of group members?

3. The confronting dimension. This is the challenge aspect of facilitation: it is to do with raising consciousness about the group's resistances to and avoidances of things it needs to face and deal with. The facilitative question is: how shall the group's consciousness be raised about these matters?

4. The feeling dimension. This is the affective aspect of facilitation: it is to do with the management of feeling within the group. The facilitative question is: how shall the life of feeling within the group be handled?

5. The structuring dimension. This is the formal aspect of facilitation: it is to do with methods of learning, with what sort of form is given to experiences within the group and with how they are to be structured. The facilitative question is: how can the group's learning experiences be structured?

6. The valuing dimension. This is the integrity aspect of facilitation: it is to do with creating a supportive climate which honours and celebrates the personhood of group members; a climate in which they can be genuine, disclosing their reality as it is, keeping in touch with their true needs and interests. The facilitative question is: how can such a climate of personal value, integrity and respect be created?

Now these six dimensions interweave and overlap, being mutually supportive of each other. Nevertheless, I hold that each one has in practice an independent identity which will claim the facilitator's attention. They need to be distinguished from each other in thought and action to achieve effective facilitation. Yet they also need to be interrelated continuously in their application: they are to be distinguished only in order to be woven into an integrated mastery of the learning process. The challenge is to keep an eye on each dimension, and organize them all, over time, into a well-balanced whole.

What characterizes them, and the specific interventions that fall under each of them, is that they are pitched at the level of human *intention*. They are about the facilitator's purposes, about what he or she is seeking to achieve, with regard to various kinds of learning in the group. The full form of the facilitative *how* question is: given that my purpose is to elicit learning through an effect on this or that dimension, how can I go about it? Each intervention intends to achieve a certain result in a certain way.

The facilitative question

The facilitative *how* question, raised under each dimension above, has a two-part answer. One part deals with *who will decide* about the issue raised - the facilitator alone, the facilitator and the participants together, or the participants alone. And this takes us into the three political modes of facilitation, given below. The other part deals with *what intervention* is to be used in dealing with the issue. This, combined with the modes, is covered in the substantial inventory of facilitative interventions given in the main body of this book.

The three modes of facilitation: the politics of learning

Each of the above six dimensions can be handled in three different ways. It is one of these three ways which will provide the answer as to who should make decisions on each dimension. From now on, in the description of modes and interventions, I shall refer to the facilitator in the second person, as 'you'.

1. The hierarchical mode. Here you, the facilitator, direct the learning process, exercise your power over it, and do things *for* the group: you lead from the front by thinking and acting on behalf of the group. You decide on the objectives and the programme, interpret and give meaning, challenge resistances, manage group feelings, provide structures for learning and honour the claims of authentic behaviour in the group. You take full responsibility, in charge of all major decisions on all dimensions of the learning process.

2. The co-operative mode. Here you share your power over the learning process and manage the different dimensions *with* the group: you enable and guide the group to become more self-directing in the various forms of learning by conferring with them. You prompt and help group members to decide on the programme, to give meaning to experiences, to do their own confrontation, and so on. In this process, you share your own view which, though influential, is not final but one among many. Outcomes are always negotiated. You collaborate with the members of the group in devising the learning process: your facilitation is co-operative.

3. The autonomous mode. Here you respect the total autonomy of the group: you do not do things for them, or with them, but give them freedom to find their *own way*, exercising their own judgment without any intervention on your part. Without any reminders, guidance or assistance, they evolve their programme, give meaning to what is going on, find ways of confronting their avoidances, and so on. The bedrock of learning is unprompted, self-directed practice, and here you give space for it. This does not mean the abdication of responsibility. It is the subtle art of creating conditions within which people can exercise full self-determination in their learning.

These three modes deal with the politics of learning, with the exercise of power in the management of the different dimensions of experience. They are about who controls and influences such management. *Who makes the decisions* about what people learn and how they learn it: the facilitator alone, the facilitator and group members together, or the group members alone? The three modes comprise a higher order, political dimension which runs through all the basic six.

As an effective facilitator, you are someone who can use all these three modes on each of the six dimensions as and when appropriate; and are flexible in moving from mode to mode and dimension to dimension in the light of the changing situation in the group. This is no doubt a counsel of perfection, but it broadens the facilitative imagination to entertain the total 18-part grid of options in the back of the mind, as in figure 1.2.

	Planning	Meaning	Confronting	Feeling	Structuring	Valuing
Hierarchy						
Co-operation						
Autonomy						

Figure 1.2 *Dimensions and modes*

Too much hierarchical control, and participants become passive and dependent or hostile and resistant. They wane in self-direction - which is the core of all learning. Too much co-operative guidance may degenerate into a subtle kind of nurturing oppression, and may deny the group the benefits of totally autonomous learning. Too much autonomy for participants and laissez-faire on your part, and they may wallow in ignorance, misconception and chaos.

The modes can include each other. You can be basically hierarchical, but with elements of co-operation and autonomy. Thus, within hierarchically given exercises, members will always be autonomous, self-directing in active practice when taking their turn. This is the heart of learning particular skills and awarenesses. Alternatively, the group as a whole may be in an autonomous phase, and call you in to do a piece of hierarchical work, etc.

The use of the modes: stages and presumptions

Each experiential group, depending on its learning objectives, will require a different balance of the three modes. And any given group may need this balance to change at different stages in its development, each stage depending on certain presumptions. The three stages below are not a formula for any learning group. It all depends on the objectives and the prior experience of group members.

Some groups, especially those attending in-service training courses for skilled people, may start at stage 2 or stage 3. But the three stages given here are classic ones for training absolute beginners, as they are for parenting. It is important to remember they can overlap, the earlier ones running on, in reduced form, beside the later ones.

1. Hierarchy early on. At the outset a clear hierarchical framework may be needed within which early development of co-operation and autonomy can occur. The presumption here is that participants are insecure and dependent in the area of learning, with lack of knowledge and skill, and have little ability therefore to orientate themselves. They will benefit from your command of events. There is also the presumption that your use of the hierarchical mode, making decisions for the learners, is based on their consent. Within the hierarchical framework, there will of course be autonomous practice and co-operative exchanges with you.

2. Co-operation mid-term. In the middle phase, more open collaboration with group members may be appropriate in managing the learning process. You negotiate the curriculum with them and co-operatively guide their learning activities. The presumption here is that they have acquired some confidence in the area of learning, with a foundation of knowledge and skill. In this way, they are able to orientate themselves and participate with you in decisions about how the learning should proceed.

3. Autonomy later on. In the later phase, much more delegation and scope for the group to be autonomous and self-directed may be needed, with peer learning contracts and self- and peer assessment. The presumption here is that group members have considerable confidence in the area of learning and have acquired evident competence in a sizeable body of knowledge and skill. They benefit from full self-determination in their learning.

Participation in educational decision-making: the classic dilemma

People in our society carry around a lot of unprocessed distress caused by having been the victims of oppressive educational methods from the earliest years - both at home and at school - where their needs and rights as embryonic persons have not been fully honoured or realised. One result of this oppression is that they lack certain basic human skills: skills in handling their own feelings, skills in interacting with other persons, skills in self-direction and collective decision-making. There has been a gross deficiency in the range and depth of their education and training.

This leads to the classic dilemma of all educational reform: students have the need and the right to be released from oppressive forms of education and should be encouraged to participate in educational decision-making; but they are beset by repressed distress, and may not have the personal, interpersonal and self-directing skills required. So they may be neither effective nor satisfied when encouraged to co-operate with you and be participative.

The resolution of this dilemma lies in mastery of the three modes and the three classic stages outlined in the preceding section on page 18. Only give away an appropriate amount of power at a time, otherwise neither you nor the students will be able to cope. And realize the huge array of options you have in combining the three modes in different ways, with varying degrees of emphasis, in relation to so many diverse facets of the educational process. There is no need to hasten inappropriately forward by gross leaps, when you can proceeed slowly by innumerable subtle steps.

The many forms of autonomy

The autonomous mode I have defined above as you, the facilitator, giving space for unprompted self-directed learning activity in the group. But this occurrence of autonomy can take place in two ways. It can be *given by you* to the group, put forward directively, in the hierarchical mode, or by negotiation, in the co-operative mode; or it can be *seized from you* by the group - participants turn the tables, reverse the roles, and become the hierarchs who divest you of your presumption to control and negotiate. Such a learning revolution, if it occurs, is a critical - and potentially fruitful - turning point in the history of a group.

There is also the obvious distinction between individual autonomy and group autonomy. They can be at odds: what I choose may conflict with the consensus choice among my self-directing peers, who thus become my controlling hierarchs, directing my action. Therefore group autonomy does not necessarily guarantee the autonomy of every one of its members.

Finally, you can delegate leadership, or delegate without leadership. The former means that you direct, or negotiate with, someone to be the acting group leader while you step out of the role. This is done either as a special exercise for skills-building in training group facilitators, or as part of general group process and group dynamic learning. If you delegate without leadership, this means that you give space for a self-directed peer group.

Task and process in experiential learning

The distinction between task and process is most obvious when the task is to bring about change in the environment. If a group is busy making a pyramid out of the furniture in the room, this is its task. The social phenomena that go on during this task, constitute the group's process: they can be described in relative independence of the task - how leadership and other roles are allocated, how decisions are made, how commmunication networks and contribution rates become established, what psychodynamic interactions between people and intrapsychic states within each person are evident, and so on.

The distinction still holds in personal development work or interactive skills training. The task is to re-enact some bit of your past in a psychodrama, or to practise some skill in a certain situation within a role play; the process is to do with the intrapsychic and interpersonal phenomena that go on as warp to the woof of the task. Here it is still possible to describe process issues independently of task issues, but although the two are distinct they lend themselves readily to being interdefinable.

The distinction is collapsed when the task of the group is to explore its own emerging process - as in a traditional sensitivity training group. Then there are two levels of process: there is the process, not being explored or attended to, that is involved in exploring the process that is being attended to. Hence any pure process group has an ever-present temptation to disappear along the recondite, infinite regress: foreground process 1, having as its background process 2, which when it is brought into the foreground will have as its background process 3, etc.

If we now bring in the concept of learning, then there are three areas for it: learning about the task; learning about the group process; and learning about the learning process itself. The last of these means understanding what is involved in getting to understand the task or the process: upper-level learning about ground-floor learning.

Of the four sorts of learning mentioned earlier, let us take the two most commonly considered: conceptual learning (about something) which can be expressed in statements; and practical learning (how to do something) which can only be expressed in terms of some practical skill. For example, to learn about group process is to understand it and to be able to make informed statements about it; to learn how to do, i.e. participate in, group process is evident in the learner's intrapersonal and interpersonal skills.

So if we put all these notions together, we get the table in figure 1.3: the four empty boxes on the left are first-order or ground-floor learning; the eight empty boxes on the right are second-order, upper-level learning.

	Task	Process	Learn(ing) about Task	Learn(ing) how to: Task	Learn(ing) about Process	Learn(ing) how to: Process
Learning about						
Learning how to:						

Figure 1.3 *Sorts and levels of learning*

So if we take the bottom row, there is learning how to do the task, learning how to handle process, learning how to learn about the task, learning how to learn how to do the task, learning how to learn about process, and learning how to learn how to handle process.

The concept of facilitator style

Facilitator style, in my view, transcends rules and principles of practice, although it takes them into account and is guided by them. There are good and bad methods of facilitating any given group, but there is no one right and proper method. There are innumerable valid approaches, each bearing the signature of different, idiosyncratic facilitators.

By facilitator style, I mean the unique way a person leads a certain group, and more generally, the distinctive way that person leads any group. We can analyse the style in terms of the dimensions, modes and particular interventions given in this book, and how these are put together. We can also see it as a function of the facilitator's values and norms, psychological make-up, degree of skill and development, of the objectives and composition of the group, and of a wider cultural context. But in the last analysis it is you, the imponderable person, that determines your style.

So there is a crucial gap between everything in this book, and the generation of your style: it can only be filled by the unique, distinctive process of your creative and selective imagination.

One-to-one, one-to-some and one-to-all interventions

This account of facilitation was originally developed out of my *Six Category Intervention Analysis*, first published in 1975, and now in a revised and enlarged third edition (Heron, 1989). The six category model is used for training one-to-one practitioners, whereas this facilitator style model is entirely for training those who lead groups.

Nevertheless, the two models usefully go together: the group facilitator will frequently have one-to-one interactions with a group member, and will then use many of the six category interventions, especially the very specific catalytic and cathartic ones, some of which I have included in this book. In what follows, I shall assume your familiarity with the six category system, and at some points will refer you to it. Lack of such familiarity, however, will not limit your understanding.

In the text, I have included, across the dimensions and modes, a mixture of interventions. There are those that relate to all of the group, those that relate to some of the group; and there are a few that relate only to one of the group, where such interventions seem fairly central to what goes on in experiential groups. I must ask the reader to get used to switching between one-to-all, one-to-some, and one-to-one interventions, and their many combinations, since this is the reality of the facilitator's role.

For details of the full range of one-to-one interventions which a group facilitator will frequently use, see my *Six Category Intervention Analysis* (Heron, 1989). However, note that some basic one-to-one interventions can also be used for some or all of a group and these are included here in their one-to-some or one-to-all forms.

Education and training

The present model is for use in developing facilitators, both beginners and those with experience. The latter particularly will find it helpful in extending their skill. In a workshop setting, the model has at least three uses.

Education. To raise consciousness about the range and subtlety of options available to all facilitators and about the implications of different facilitator profiles across the dimensions and modes.

Assessment. To provide a tool for self-assessment and peer assessment, so that facilitators get more insight into their strengths and weaknesses.

Training. To provide the basis for a set of exercises that build up skill both within particular dimensions and modes, and within a selected profile across the dimensions and modes.

I assume throughout this book an educational model for experiential learning groups of all kinds, including psychotherapy groups and personal development groups. Whatever the sort of group, its members are acquiring new understanding of themselves and others, and new skills in managing their own process and in relating to others. To extend education into personal development and the management of feelings, social skills, decision-making, and the combinations of these, makes it truly *education for living*.

The 18 basic options

I conclude this chapter with an overview of the dimensions and modes combined into the 18 basic options for the group facilitator. This gives a summary outline of the content of Chapters 3 to 8 inclusive. For convenience, I have numbered each option as in the following figure:

	Planning	Meaning	Confronting	Feeling	Structuring	Valuing
Hierarchy	1	4	7	10	13	16
Co-operation	2	5	8	11	14	17
Autonomy	3	6	9	12	15	18

Figure 1.4 *Dimensions and modes*

Don't be misled by the simplified statement of each option. The different modes within each dimension are not mutually exclusive: they can all be used on the same course, at different times, and with respect to different aspects of the given dimension.

1. The planning dimension: hierarchical mode. You here plan *for* the group: you direct the planning of the group's learning, deciding unilaterally on the content of the course programme and making decisions for the learners.

2. The planning dimension: co-operative mode. You plan the programme *with* the group: you are committed to negotiate, to take into account and seek agreement with the views of group members in constructing the timetable.

3. The planning dimension: autonomous mode. You delegate the planning of the programme *to* the group: you are getting out of the way, affirming the group's need to work out its own course design.

4. The meaning dimension: hierarchical mode. You make sense of what is going on *for* the group: you give meaning to events and illuminate them; you are the source of understanding what is going on.

5. The meaning dimension: co-operative mode. You invite group members to participate *with* you in the generation of understanding: you prompt them to give their own meaning to what is happening in the group, then add your view, as one idea among others, and collaborate in making sense.

6. The meaning dimension: autonomous mode. You choose to delegate interpretation, feedback, reflection and review *to* the group: making sense of what is going on is autonomous, entirely self-generated within the group.

7. The confronting dimension: hierarchical mode. You interrupt the rigid behaviour, point to what is being avoided, and do this directly *to* people and *for* people - in such a way that those concerned may take up the issue and thereby show some awareness of their avoidance.

8. The confronting dimension: co-operative mode. You work *with* the group and its members to raise consciousness about avoided issues and defensive behaviour: you prompt, invite and ask people, consult them, compare and share views with them. Consciousness-raising is collaborative.

9. The confronting dimension: autonomous mode. You now hand over all consciousness-raising about defensive, avoidance behaviour *to* the group: you create a climate and learning structures which enable group members to practise self- and peer confrontation.

10. The feeling dimension: hierarchical mode. You take full charge of the emotional dynamic of the group *for* the group, directing its process and deciding how it will be handled: you think for group members, judging what methods of managing feelings will suit them and their purposes best.

11. The feeling dimension: co-operative mode. You work *with* the group, eliciting, prompting, and encouraging views, discussing with members different ways of handling feelings: you practise collaborative management of the emotional dynamic of the group.

12. The feeling dimension: autonomous mode. You give the group space for - and delegate *to* it - the process of managing its own emotional dynamic.

13. The structuring dimension: hierarchical mode. You structure learning activities *for* the group: you design the exercises and directively supervise their use by the group.

14. The structuring dimension: co-operative mode. You structure learning methods *with* group members, co-operating with them in devising how the learning shall proceeed: they collaborate with you in designing the structured exercises, and in supervising the running of them.

15. The structuring dimension: autonomous mode. You delegate *to* group members control over their own learning process: they are entirely self- and peer directed in the design of structured exercises, and in supervising the running of them.

16. The valuing dimension: hierarchical mode. You take strong initiatives to care *for* group members: you manifest directly to them, in word and deed, your commitment to their fundamental worth as persons.

17. The valuing dimension: co-operative mode. You create a community of value and mutual respect *with* group members: you are inclusive and interactive, collaborating with them as all emerge as self-creating persons.

18. The valuing dimension: autonomous mode. You choose to delegate the affirmation of self-worth *to* group members, giving them space to celebrate the value of personal identity and emergence in their own way.

Criteria of validity

This whole system of dimensions and modes is pitched at the level of human intention. It maps the range of purposes out of which facilitators can create their style. As such, and as with any account of human intention and purpose, it presupposes some very general values and norms. Therefore its validity is, in part, to do with its moral justification. What are the ethical values and principles that underlie it, and are these sound?

Its validity is also, in part, phenomenological: the system articulates options relevant in the current human world, and in this respect it involves a radical empiricism (Heron, 1988b) - an experiential awareness of the basic phenomenal categories that make sense of what is going on in the facilitation of group learning. It is open to any experientially sensitive group participant or facilitator to engage in this kind of phenomenological inquiry.

There are obvious logical criteria involved in its validity. Is the system comprehensive and inclusive of all the main parameters? Is it internally coherent, are the main elements consistent with each other? And, whatever the degrees of interdependence and overlap, are the main elements relatively independent of each other?

Each reader can apply these criteria in the light of personal reflection and experience. For their corporate and systematic use, the research paradigm of co-operative inquiry (Reason, 1988) offers a powerful way forward .

2. The group dynamic

By the group dynamic I mean the combined configuration of mental, emotional and physical energy in the group at any given time; and the way this configuration undergoes change. I will first look at stages of the group dynamic; sketch in some of its positive forms; give considerable attention to the negative forms, and outline the role of the facilitator in dealing with them; and finally consider some further dimensions of group dynamic theory.

Stages of the group dynamic

There is no reliable rule about how the dynamic will develop and unfold through the history of a group. The configuration of its energies can take many different forms, both positive and negative. The positive forms are usually attained after a passage through the negative forms. This attainment will depend on the objectives of the group, its programme, its membership, and the role of the facilitator. Later in this chapter I consider seven kinds of positive form: task-oriented, process-oriented, expressive, interactive, confronting, personal work oriented, charismatic. And three kinds of negative form: the educationally alienated, the culturally restricted and the psychologically defensive.

Although the total history of the group dynamic is variable, depending on the factors I have just mentioned, one can pick out four more obvious phases, so far as the shift from negative to positive forms is concerned. There is a cyclic flow of energy, as through the four seasons of the year from the time of the winter solstice.

1. The stage of defensiveness. This is usually at the outset of a group. Trust is low, anxiety is high, the group dynamic may get locked into one or more of the three restricted forms - educationally alienated, culturally restricted, psychologically defensive - described later in this chapter. Wintertime: the ground may be frozen, and the weather stormy.

2. The stage of working through defensiveness. The group is now under way, trust is building, anxiety is reducing, as the facilitator is busy with the kind of strategies presented in this book. A fresh culture is being created. Springtime: new life starts to break through the surface crust.

3. The stage of authentic behaviour. The group is deep into its real destiny. Trust is high, and anxiety is a spur to growth and change. There is openness to self and others, risk-taking, working, caring and sharing. There is flexibility in moving between different strands of learning. Leadership is shared, with a good balance of hierarchy, co-operation and autonomy. Authentic behaviour has many varieties and can include any of the positive forms of the group dynamic - task-oriented, process-oriented, expressive, interactive, confronting, personal work oriented, charismatic - described in the next section below. Summertime: there is an abundance of growth, and the sun is high.

4. Closure. As the group draws to a close, the members gather in and review the fruit of their learning, and prepare to transfer it to life in the wider world outside. At some point in this process separation anxiety will loom up - the distress at parting after such trust and depth of interaction. It can slip the group back into defensiveness unless dealt with awarely - firstly by accepting that the end is nigh, secondly by dealing with any unfinished business, thirdly by celebrating each other and what has gone on, fourthly by saying a warm, friendly farewell in the group and one-to-one. Autumn: the fruit is harvested and stored, the harvesters give thanks and go their way.

Positive forms of the group dynamic

The whole purpose of this book is to help these forms come into being. The facilitator's concern is to enable them to emerge through the *Sturm und Drang* of the negative forms.

1. Task-oriented. The group is outgoing, busy with the experiential learning cycle, practising some particular skill, undergoing some experience, exploring some issue. Members co-operate in learning, in problem-solving and decision-making. When the group is using the *experiential learning cycle,* it either grounds thought in action, encounter, and practice; or distils thought out of these components of experience. So there are two complementary versions of the cycle. The first starts with a concept, cashes it out in appropriate experience, then reviews the concept in the light of so grounding it. The second starts with a certain kind of experience, distils a mental model out of this, then takes the model back into experience to develop and refine it.

2. Process-oriented. The group is ingoing, examining its own psychosocial process, seeking to understand *how* it is functioning.

3. Expressive. The group is active with celebration and creative expression in word, art, music, song or movement.

4. Interactive. Group members are engaged in interpersonal work and feedback, giving and receiving impressions, sharing attractions and aversions, withdrawing and owning projections.

5. Confronting. Members are engaged in creative conflict resolution, in supportive confrontation.

6. Personal work oriented. Individual members are taking time for personal growth work. Each one has a turn, working in pairs or small groups, or with you in the presence of the whole group. This work covers a wide spectrum, from cognitive and analytic self-discovery, through emotional disclosure, regression and catharsis, to imaginal or ritual transmutation and transpersonal development.

7. Charismatic. The group is attuning to psychic and spiritual energies, entering altered states of consciousness and action.

Where the positive forms abound, group members have adaptibility in moving between different strands of learning and experience. Similarly, the facilitator has flexibility in moving between the six dimensions, and has the right balance of hierarchy, co-operation and autonomy.

In more general terms, these seven positive forms can be seen as the outcome of three main influences: *cultural liberation* - avant-garde ideas, practices, norms and values from the growing edge of the surrounding culture that come into the group via the facilitator and forward-thinking group members; *educational confluence* - different strands and kinds of learning, alongside each other and interacting; *psychological openness* - the willingness of group members to open up to the challenge of change and growth. These are shown in figure 2.1 below.

Cultural liberation - the influence of innovative thought and practice from outside - manifests through the ideas and skill of the facilitator, which generate educational confluence - holism in course design and method. This in turn sets the scene for the psychological openness of course participants. The facilitator, through command of the educational process, mediates between cultural progress and individual learning and growth.

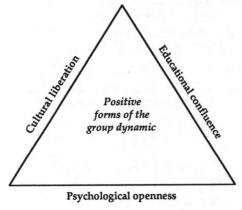

Figure 2.1 *Influences on positive forms*

Negative forms of the group dynamic

The counterparts to this positive triad are three main kinds of negative form, each with sub-varieties. These are shown in figure 2.2. They interlock, affecting and influencing each other. You could say they are three different but overlapping perspectives on the same basic phenomenon: a block, a rigidity, a restriction in the dynamic of the group, so that learning is distorted or held back.

1. Educational alienation. The group is limited to just one kind of learning objective. Its dynamic becomes contracted, cut off from other kinds of being and learning.

2. Cultural oppression. Group behaviour is restricted by oppressive norms, values and beliefs that flow into it and permeate it from the surrounding culture.

3. Psychological defensiveness. Group behaviour is distorted by the various anxieties of participants: present and past distress floods the group dynamic, throwing it into rigid, defensive forms.

Oppressive beliefs and practices from the culture are manifest in the limited and alienating educational model used within the course, and both set the scene for the psychological defensiveness of course participants. I will now consider each of these three factors in more detail.

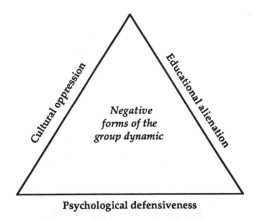

Psychological defensiveness

Figure 2.2 *Influences on negative forms*

Educational alienation

Learning objectives of the group

What the group is for, that is, what its members have come together to learn and do, will influence the configuration of group energies. Different objectives will have different effects. A comprehensive account of learning objectives can be derived from six basic areas of human experience.

1. Economic/practical. The objective of the group is to learn some technical or manual skills for application in productive or service occupations, or in allied hobbies.

2. Intellectual/theoretical. The group is busy with intellectual learning of either pure or applied knowledge.

3. Political/organizational. The group is learning human relations and other skills for managing and changing social, economic and political structures.

4. Aesthetic. The group is learning skills in artistic creation or interpretation.

5. Transpersonal. The group is learning skills in entering altered states of consciousness - psychic, charismatic, meditative and spiritual states.

6. Personal/interpersonal. The group is learning skills in both personal development and in interacting with other people.

7. Composite. The group is combining two or more of the above sorts of learning objectives.

Each of the first six can have different effects on the group dynamic. But these effects have a common underlying form: they each involve some sort of *alienation*. It is not that this alienation is necessarily going to occur. But there is a tendency for it to happen where the learning objectives of the group are *single-stranded*.

Alienated forms of the group dynamic

Alienation is to do with dissociation, fragmentation, separation, being cut off, indifferent, remote and estranged. It can occur within a person, as self-alienation, when that person becomes identified with some aspect of the self and cut off from other aspects. And it can occur between people, so that people relate to each other in a closed, restricted and estranged kind of way. To clarify: the alienation *of* A *from* B, means that A is developed in a way that excludes and is cut off from the development of B.

1. Alienation of intellect. In a group pursuing only intellectual objectives, the group dynamic can suffer alienation: the mental activity in the group gets cut off from emotional and physical realities, interactions between people become excessively cognitive and emotionally dead or indifferent. Talk is all in terms of generalities and the outside world, far removed from personal experience.

2. Alienation of affect. In a group committed to personal and interpersonal development objectives, the reverse kind of alienation can occur: the group gets immersed in a turgid emotional life of shared experience, cut off from the exercise of reflection and thought, and so does not understand or make enough sense of what is going on. Interaction is in terms of immediate felt experience, far removed from more comprehensive perspectives.

The dynamic in both the above kinds of group may also become quite dissociated from the spiritual dimension of being.

3. Alienation of spirit. Groups that pursue purely transpersonal learning objectives, may share personal spiritual experiences, but in the process become alienated from adequate intellectual discrimination and also from emotional realities and authentic interpersonal openness.

4. Alienation from the body. Each of the above three kinds of group may in their different ways and to differing degrees become alienated from the body, its energies, sensations and impulses, especially its need to be owned, identified and enjoyed as an expressive form of the psyche - mind, feelings and spirit - in space.

A group with a single-stranded set of learning objectives is prone to an alienated dynamic: once it has launched itself unawarely on only one kind of learning, it will get stuck there. It makes sense to design an experiential group with composite, multi-stranded objectives, so that it may develop a non-alienated dynamic. This means, for example, combining intellectual, personal, interpersonal and transpersonal objectives in the same group: one of these may be the primary strand of learning, with the other three acting as complementary strands.

Educational alienation, therefore, is to be dealt with primarily at the stage of course design. This is supported by effective facilitation of switching between different strands of learning as the course unfolds.

The overall goal is holistic learning, many threads interweaving, or, to change the metaphor, confluent education - many streams running side by side with interconnecting channels. In this way, the physical body, the energy system, the feelings, the intellect, the will and the spiritual powers can be integrated and developed in varying combinations in the process of growth and learning.

Cultural oppression

The cultural context

The participants of the group are enrolled from the surrounding culture. They bring with them, embedded in their attitudes and behaviour, many of the restrictive values and norms of that culture. Unless confronted and transformed, these will become the tacit values and norms of the group. I will select one prevailing cultural value and one prevailing cultural norm.

1. Competitiveness. The culture fosters the value of competition - for profit, possessions, pleasure, status, competence and power.

2. Emotional closure. The culture has a powerful norm of controlling and suppressing feelings of all kinds. It accepts only a limited expression of positive feelings and expects the total repression of distress feelings.

Both these will pervade the group in its early stages and will impose a related set of social restrictions on behaviour in the group.

Socially restricted forms of the group dynamic

There are many of these. I identify some of the more obvious ones that can all occur in a group of beginners. They are less likely in an advanced group, although one can never count on this.

1. Rigid contribution hierarchy. By a contribution rate I mean the degree to which any one person speaks in the group. A number of high contributors emerge fairly swiftly, verbally dominating the proceedings. There are others with a medium contribution rate and a residual number who are low contributors or who never say anything at all.

A contribution hierarchy will function with great persistence and lack of awareness, unless broken up. A variety of discussion procedures can achieve this break.

2. Power struggles. A contribution hierarchy can also turn into a decision hierarchy, in which high contributors struggle with each other to railroad through their preferred choices. Democratic decision-procedures are needed to deal with this.

3. Gender bias. This is changing in the surrounding culture, but is still extensive. It can invade the group: men speak and act first, often interrupting women without realizing, verbally elbowing them out of the way. Women's needs, perspectives and initiatives are ignored or suppressed and the women let this happen.

4. Compulsive task-orientation. There will be a strong compulsion to fill unscheduled or process-oriented time with some clearly defined, easily identified and familiar kind of task.

5. Emotional and physical isolation. There is a very strong tacit norm that people keep emotionally buttoned-up and physically entirely separate. Self-disclosure about certain kinds of personal information and emotion is taboo, as is any kind of touching or holding of other people.

These socially restricted forms yield somewhat to consciousness-raising at their own level. Helping group members to become aware of these and other cultural invasions is an important part of the learning process.

They interact intimately, however, with the psychological defensive forms, which are discussed below, so both forms need to be dealt with alongside each other.

Psychological defensiveness

The anxieties of participants

The dynamic of a group is strongly influenced by the anxieties of its participants. Such collective tension obscures the route to experiential learning. At the outset of a group, there is an abundance of disquiet just below the surface of the group dynamic. This anxiety is of two basic kinds: *existential* and *archaic*.

1. Existential anxiety. This anxiety arises out of the immediate situation of being in the group. The participant at the start of an experiential learning course has, to a greater or lesser degree which partly depends on their experience of the method, an identity crisis. This has three interconnected components which reinforce each other, in the individual and *collectively*.

Acceptance anxiety. Will I be accepted, liked, wanted? Or will I be rejected, disliked and unwanted? Here the person's need to love and be loved is at risk.

Orientation anxiety. Will I understand what is going on? Will I be able to make sense of this situation, so that I can find some kind of identity within it? Here the person's need to understand and be understood is at risk.

Performance anxiety. Will I be able to do what I have come to learn? Will I be competent or incompetent? Will I be able to control the situation to meet my needs? Here the person's need to act and choose, the need for mastery and personal power, is at risk.

These are all perfectly normal and healthy fears. On their own, if modest, they may act as spurs to fulfilment, motivating members, respectively, to find acceptance with others, make sense of their experience and perform well in the given tasks. If this is so, then their influence on the group dynamic is positive and benign, helping to create a co-operative, meaningful and constructive climate. But if they become stronger, they may distort the group dynamic into relatively minor defensive forms that can impede learning.

However, existential anxiety may also be compounded by archaic anxiety. Either the existential anxiety becomes very strong and triggers the archaic or it is high because the archaic is already running into it. The group dynamic may then be flooded by more fear than anyone can handle. The behaviour of participants is distorted into major defensive forms, the compound anxiety being displaced into unaware, maladaptive attitudes that entirely block learning and growth.

2. Archaic anxiety. This anxiety is the presenting symptom, on the fringe of consciousness, of the repressed distress of the past - the personal hurt, particularly of childhood, that .has been denied so that the individual can survive emotionally. The undischarged pain of this much earlier and more radical identity crisis, is precipitated toward the surface, stirred up by the existential anxiety of being in the group, and beyond this by certain threatening issues, which I discuss in the next section.

Archaic anxiety represents three interconnected forms of repressed distress which all have their roots in traumatic childhood situations and their elaboration from later experiences of hurt and oppression:

Repressed grief. The hidden pain of not having received and not having been able to give enough love: the pain of emotional rejection, deprivation and neglect.

Repressed fear. The hidden panic of having felt that one's whole identity is being threatened by overwhelming situations one cannot understand, control or resist.

Repressed anger. The buried rage at the interference with one's liberty, one's freedom to explore oneself and the world in the light of one's own imagination, needs and interests.

There are less and much more severe forms of these three. Most people seem to carry around some degree of each. This is because we live in an emotionally repressive culture, in which social conditioning requires children to learn to suppress, ignore and eventually deny their personal hurts - rather than find healing through catharsis and awareness training (Heron, 1983).

On top of the deeper repressions of grief, fear and anger, there is a much more accessible kind of archaic distress - *embarrassment*, which is basically a conditioned fear of what people will think if they find out about the real you. It acts as a powerful inhibitor of the underlying pain.

Threatening issues

There are certain threatening issues which arise at different stages of a group's history. In the early stages of a group, these issues will tend to be more disturbing than in later stages. They are threatening not only because they generate existential anxiety, but even more so because they can stir up archaic anxiety which then starts to run into and reinforce the existential disquiet. These issues are typically to do with authority and control; conflict and aggression; intimacy and contact; love and care; sexuality and gender; identity and purpose; disclosure and expression; truth and honesty; mastery and competence; knowledge and ignorance. Such themes, when they arise at a certain time and in a certain way in the group, may resonate with the earliest, most vulnerable and often traumatic experiences of early life.

Then archaic anxiety comes to the fore, triggered directly by the threatening issue itself, or by a build up in the existential anxiety which that issue arouses. When the archaic is on the move, and tangles with the existential, the total charge of tension can become disabling. The group dynamic is distorted into certain typical defensive forms. Existential anxiety on its own, when strong enough, can also generate these forms, but in a much less severely distorted form.

Defensive forms of the group dynamic

There seems to be a collusion, a contagion, an unconscious kind of triggering mediated by subliminal cues, so that at times the whole group is locked in the defensive mode. The defence is against both the threatening issue, and the provoked anxiety with its underlying existential and archaic agendas.

The group dynamic can then have three defensive forms which can be mutually reinforcing and which can co-exist - in different sub-groups - at the same time.

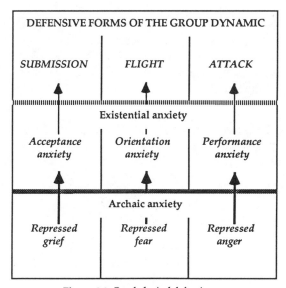

Figure 2.3 *Psychological defensiveness*

1. Submission. Group members displace their anxiety into a family of distorted passive behaviours. They may become compulsively dependent on the group leader, or any rival leader, blindly following, seeking permission. They may show signs of withdrawal and shut-down, of powerlessness, loss of identity and of compulsive guilt. They are inwardly isolated, alienated, and constrained by tacit norms that inhibit intimacy, emotion and contact.

2. Flight. The anxiety is displaced into compulsive flight. The indications are: irrelevant theorizing and generalizing; jocularity; gossip about trivialities; persistently talking about the world outside the group; 'rescuing' someone from the brink of real personal work and self-disclosure; compulsive questioning of someone in the group; retreating into a collusive pair with some other group member; insisting on a clear task, a programme, a conventional goal.

3. Attack. The anxiety is displaced into compulsive attack. The group leader is resisted, his or her proposals rejected, his or her authority, relevance or competence challenged. One or more group members may compete in a rival bid for leadership. Some group member may be scapegoated - irrationally blamed, invalidated, criticized, accused, labelled and stereotyped. The room and other physical facilities may be continuously complained about. Any positive change in the dynamic may be interrupted and wrecked. Good energy is mocked.

Figure 2.3 shows in broad outline the conceptual model of defensive forms. It simplifies the total process, of course. In reality, there are not just three vertical lines of influence as the arrows suggest, but an interlocking network of influences. Nevertheless, the arrows do pick out primary dynamic connections.

It is important to make a distinction between acute and chronic defensive forms. Acute ones are products of existential anxiety only, and have little or no significant resonance with past pain. Chronic defensive forms result from a strong charge of archaic anxiety which boosts the existential. The acute ones are much less distorted than the chronic, and will yield more readily to interruption than the chronic.

The role of the facilitator, among other things, is to help group members unlock themselves from these defensive forms, and so create a different kind of group dynamic. However, before considering this role, we must note that the facilitator can be involved in a special way in defensive forms. This brings us to transference.

Transference

When transference occurs, participants unconsciously *transfer* to the group leader, from the hurt child within, hidden and repressed feelings about a parent or some other important authority figure from the past. If the transference is positive, then the group members unconsciously project on to the facilitator the frozen need and longing for the good parent they never had. If it is negative, they project the distorted fear and anger about the bad parent they actually had.

Submissive forms of defensiveness directed at the group leader, such as dependency, following and permission-seeking, may be rooted in a positive transference. On the other hand, defensiveness that attacks the group leader, such as resistance, denigration, sabotage and rivalry, may be rooted in negative transference.

A positive transference can be put to work and used to motivate learning and growth for a period. But sooner or later the persons concerned need to withdraw - and perhaps be helped to withdraw - the projection, see it for what it is, and assume the attitudes of their own authentic adulthood. A negative transference always tends to make learning more difficult as long as it is in place, and where it is particularly strong in someone, the facilitator may need to work intensively with the person concerned, so that he or she can identify the projection and withdraw it, after being helped to release some of the underlying distress.

In the dynamic of a group it is useful to distinguish between an acute transference and a chronic one. An acute transference is one which many members may temporarily undergo at some early stage of the group: it causes them to slip into defensive behaviour for a while, but as things proceed, and with a little facilitation, they move out of it quite readily. A chronic transference, however, is one which fastens relentlessly on to the facilitator, and, as I have said, may need special and sustained attention to be resolved.

This process of unaware projection of feelings that belong to the past, on to some one or more persons in the present, is one of the most persistent phenomena in the dynamic of a group. It goes every which way, not just from member to leader, but from member to member. In this case, it widens out beyond feelings for parents and authority figures: any kind of repressed distress about anyone from the past can be unawarely projected on to some present person - who is thus unconsciously appointed to be the current scapegoat for past ills.

This blind scapegoating is also a defence against facing and owning and dealing with the hidden pain. Hence a strong projection will not want to let go of its victim, and may powerfully resist being seen for what it is. The deeper the hurt, the more relentless is the projection.

The unaware projection of hidden distress from the past may also proceed from the facilitator to one or more group members, or even the group as a whole. This is so-called counter-transference. Once your facilitation gets tangled up with your own blindly projected distress, it degenerates, and the group dynamic rapidly goes down the drain. One basic criterion of good facilitators is that they keep relatively clear of their past unfinished business while on the job.

The role of the facilitator

The dynamic of the group is grounded in the life of feeling. Hence in Chapter 6, which deals with the feeling dimension, I call it the emotional dynamic of the group, and look in more detail at ways of managing it directly at the feeling level. However, while it is controlled through impact on the feelings of group members, this impact can also be made indirectly through the other dimensions. The whole of the rest of this book is about different ways in which you, the facilitator, can influence it. But when it is locked into negative forms, here are some of the basic things you can do to move it on. This list anticipates strategies that will be dealt with in more detail later.

1. For educational alienation

Holistic course design. You can create a multi-stranded curriculum with learning objectives of complementary kinds. Your design combines different kinds of learning which involve and integrate different aspects of the whole person.

Effective switching. You manage effectively the switch from one strand of learning to another. This is to do with the timing of the switch - making it when it is needed; and the manner - helping people to adjust.

2. For cultural restrictions

Consciousness-raising. You seek to raise people's consciousness about contribution rates, gender bias, task compulsion, emotional isolation. You confront the restriction by identifying it and pointing it out.

Interruption. Having pointed out the restriction, you interrupt both its active and its passive forms by devising procedures and exercises that break it up; or by asking those involved to practise alternative behaviours on the spot.

3. For psychological defensiveness. Many of these will also deal with cultural restrictions, which are simply forms of psychological defensiveness in society at large.

Culture-setting. At the very beginning of the group, you gently manifest charismatic, distress-free authority in declaring values of warmth, support, trust and safety as the basic culture of the group. You affirm the worth and rights of persons.

Permission-giving. Again, with distress-free authority, you clearly give permission for people to be vulnerable, to uncover and heal their hurts.

Growth ground-rules. You propose a clear set of ground-rules that help members to overcome the more obvious defensive behaviours: speaking in the first person singular, addressing others directly, and so on.

Honouring choice. You make it clear that every group member has a right to choose when to lower their defences, and to choose when to do some personal work. You respect this in practice, never pressure anyone.

Conceptual orientation. You give a short theoretical input on the nature of existential and archaic anxiety, and the ways they can distort the group dynamic into distorted forms.

Confronting. You raise consciousness about issues being avoided, also about defensive and distorted behaviour. The latter includes transferences, i.e. projections on to you, and between group members.

Emotional switching. You deftly propose some activity that interrupts the defensive block by switching emotional energy from it, and into some other way of being. Restoring a light and positive climate, when things get too heavy.

Laughter. Keep the group bursting into laughter at regular intervals. This discharges the conditioned fear we call embarrassment, and so reduces the tendency of the dynamic to get locked into defensive forms.

Lowering the cathartic threshold. You introduce structured exercises, such as those involving breathing and body work, that interrupt body-mind defences and bring the underlying distress up for discharge and healing.

Individual work. You work with an individual in front of the group, with everyone's attention and support, showing that the release of emotional hurt is healing and restorative. This includes work on projections on to you and between group members.

Group autonomy. Not everything is to be dealt with by facilitation. The group also needs times to spot its defensive forms on its own, and find its own ways of interrupting them and getting into a working phase.

Transpersonal influences on the group dynamic

The group dynamic can become transformed and transmuted by opening it up to subtle forms of energy and spiritual influence, by means of invocation, ritual, mudras, mantras and other procedures. This takes us into the domain of the charismatic and the occult group. I have written more about this elsewhere (Heron, 1987; Heron, 1988).

Further extensions of group dynamic theory

The threatening issues which I have listed above are those that are most immediately involved in the dynamic of any face-to-face human group, and the anxieties to which they give rise - existential and archaic - are the bedrock of any group dynamic theory, in my view. But I believe there are two other kinds of anxiety, aroused by two other kinds of threatening issue - of a more wide-ranging sort.

1. **Cultural and planetary anxiety.** The issues which give rise to this are: is the society in which I live making the most of its human and physical resources? Is it a just society? Does it acknowledge fully human rights?

Are we taking care of our planet, preserving and fostering our total environment? Can we master the population explosion and global food shortage? Can we cross the divide between rich and poor nations? Can we stop the expropriation of profits from the third world? Will we destroy our planet by nuclear holocaust? How do we reduce defence budgets?

2. Transcendental anxiety. The issues which give rise to this are: what happens to me after death? Am I surrounded by another world? What is its impact upon me now? What are the great reaches of transcendental creation? Are there invisible powers and presences? How do I contact them?

Is there a god? What is my relation with such a reality? Is my soul saved, or lost, or neither? What is my destiny? How have I come into being? Who or what has made me? Am I created continuously? What is the ground of my identity? Who am I?

The most radical thesis about these two kinds of anxiety is that they provide, in their very different ways, the parameters within which existential and archaic anxiety arise. Or, to put it another way, the threatening issues which give rise to existential and archaic anxiety are themselves subordinate to the two sorts of wider issue, which give rise to cultural/planetary anxiety and transcendental anxiety. These further anxieties may also be aroused to distort the group dynamic into distinctive defensive forms, which will need attention in their own right.

Looked at in the positive mode, there are two very fundamental and complementary challenges here. On the one hand, the challenge of shaping a new kind of society, both locally and globally, which *cares* for the planetary environment; and on the other hand, the challenge of living awarely in a multi-dimensional universe. Both these challenges provide an exhilarating context for the future development and application of experiential learning.

3. The planning dimension

For you, the facilitator, the issue here is: what are the objectives of the group and its progamme of activities, and how will these be decided? The main objectives will have already been chosen by you in preparing the course. It is important to state them clearly in the pre-course publicity, so that you may reasonably assume that, when the group convenes, its members are already committed to them.

The main objectives may, however, be chosen by other people in the organization for which you work as a trainer. In which case, you need to think clearly whether they are ones you can truly make you own. If so, fine; if not, then you will wish to make sure there is some way of negotiating changes in them. And if you can't get the changes you want, then you have to decide whether the issues are trivial or the stuff of which resignations are made.

Much of the programme may also be planned and decided by you because that may be appropriate to the kind of group it is, as in some special skills training for beginners. But as group members take these skills on board, then at some point they have a claim to be consulted about further planning. The more autonomous they become in the mastery of a new range of skills, the more *they* know about how they need to develop them in the future.

In other groups, such as those for in-service further training, it may be appropriate to adopt consultative planning from the outset, because the participants have a good understanding of what they need to learn, and their experience needs to be honoured. However, from the standpoint of your specialist knowledge, you also have an important perspective on what experienced professionals need to learn.

As we will see later, some consultative planning is ultimately hierarchical, in that you the facilitator retain the power of final veto and decide what to accept or reject among participants' proposals. And some is genuinely co-operative, in that you claim no such power and negotiate the final outcome.

When to plan for the group, plan with the group, or give space to the group to plan on its own? It depends on the sort of group - its learning objectives; the length of the group - how long it lasts; the level of learning and experience in the group members; and the stage in group development - whether early, mid-term, or later on.

Whenever you consult a group about its programme of learning, you are implicitly asking its members to identify their personal learning needs and goals and so to make sure that the programme will fulfil them. You may want to make this process explicit, and precede any consultation with an exercise in which each person assesses their own learning needs. Please bear this in mind when you read the words 'consult' or 'consultation' below.

Planning overview

If we consider the total educational process, there are four key areas for planning:

1. Objectives. These give an account of what group members will learn from the course: the main sorts of insight, knowledge, skills, changes of state and being to be acquired.

2. Programme. This is the timetable for realizing the objectives. It distributes all the topics over time, allocating resources and indicating methods. I discuss this in more detail below.

3. Assessment. This is to determine whether group members have realized the learning objectives through participation in the programme. It requires criteria of competence or achievement, a method for applying these criteria to the learners' performance, and a way of deciding the final assessment outcome.

4. Evaluation. This is to evaluate the facilitator's style and competence and all aspects of the programme and of the assessment procedures.

If we take the three decision-modes of hierarchy, co-operation and autonomy - you, the facilitator, decide unilaterally for the group, decide bilaterally with the group, and delegate decision-making to the group - then we have the table of options shown in figure 3.1.

	Objectives	Programme	Assessment	Evaluation
Hierarchy: *you alone*				
Co-operation: *you with group*				
Autonomy: *group alone*				

Figure 3.1 *The modes in educational decision-making*

There are very many ways of *combining* the decision-modes going across the table. Thus you alone may decide on the learning objectives and on the course programme, co-operate with the group in deciding assessment procedures, and let the group alone do the course evaluation. There are also many ways of combining the decision-modes within one column. So some parts of the course programme you plan alone, some parts you plan with the group, and some parts the group plans on its own. Combining options both across and within columns gives you enormous scope in the politics of educational decision-making.

Now let us take one of the four items considered above: the course programme.The main elements of a programme of learning are:

1. Topics. These cover the range of subject matter, of what is to be learned, in each of the different strands of the curriculum. The programme will contain certain basic sorts of topic, and within each sort, a detailed set of contents.

2. Time. The programme distributes the topics over time. There are several aspects to this: the total length of the programme; the total number of hours for each sort of topic; the sequence of topics, those which come before, those which come after, and those which run concurrently, side by side.

3. Resources. These include human resources of two main kinds: staff and other students, and physical resources: books, articles, computers, lab equipment, rooms, and so on.

4. Methods. These include teaching and learning methods, their integration in the facilitation of learning, and various methods for assessing student performance.

Again, if we take the three decision-modes of hierarchy, co-operation and autonomy - you, the facilitator, decide unilaterally for the group, decide bilaterally with the group, and delegate decision-making to the group - then we have the following table of options with respect to planning the course programme, as shown in figure 3.2.

	Topics	Time	Resources	Methods
Hierarchy: *you alone*				
Co-operation: *you with group*				
Autonomy: *group alone*				

Figure 3.2 *The modes in programme planning*

Here too there are very many ways of combining the decision-modes going across the table. Thus you alone may decide on the range of topics, co-operate with the group in deciding the use of resources and teaching /learning methods, and let the group alone work out the time issues of length, sequencing, and pacing. There are also many ways of combining the decision-modes within one column. So some teaching/learning methods you decide on alone, some you decide with the group, and some the group determines for itself. Again, combining options both across and within columns gives enormous scope in the politics of programme planning.

What now follows is a basic map of political options for you as facilitator of learning. Figure 3.3 shows the seven ways of using the decision-modes, singly and in various combinations. It applies to the four educational components of learning objectives, course programme, student assessment, course evaluation; and to the four elements within a course programme of topics, time, resources and methods. Remember that 'all' and 'some' in the table below refer to items both *across* columns and *within* columns in the previous tables.

	Hierarchy	Co-operation	Autonomy
1.	*You decide all*		
2.	*You decide some*	*You with group decide some*	
3.	*You decide some*	*You with group decide some*	*Group decide some*
4.	*You decide some*		*Group decide some*
5.		*You with group decide some*	*Group decide some*
6.		*You with group decide all*	
7.			*Group decide all*

Figure 3.3 *Seven ways of using decision-modes in planning*

Let us consider this table in relation to the fundamental components of objectives, programe, assessment and evaluation. Row 1 is the traditional, authoritarian model of education: staff decide everything - what the students shall learn, how they shall learn it and whether they have learnt it. Row 7 is the peer self-help model of education, where there are no staff and you have no facilitator role: this is the entirely autonomous, self-directed group.

Rows 5 and 6 are dubious: they imply that absolutely everything is up for negotiation and, in row 5, delegation. But if *everything* really is negotiable, you do not stand for anything, have no educational model on offer. If you have really thought through the matter, there will be some aspects of the educational process which will be non-negotiable because they exemplify values and principles to which you are committed. These aspects define the sort of educational model you are dedicated to realize.

Thus your model may include significant student participation with staff in educational decision-making. And your commitment to this makes it a non-negotiable principle, stated in the course prospectus, to which new students are invited to subscribe. You are not open to people on your course negotiating you back into authoritarian, unilateral decision-making.

Row 3 is the most comprehensive educational model. It combines all the decision-modes, and provides the greatest scope for the effective facilitation of learning. It represents the view that hierarchy - in certain forms, at certain stages and applied in certain areas - is a necessary condition for the embryonic development of self-determination. This is the paradox: that people need to be led to freedom, to be guided and taught to be autonomous.

Levels of decision-making

Implicit in the previous section are three levels of decision-making. I will consider them here in relation to the course programme.

1. Choosing decision-modes for planning. This is planning how to plan. It involves choosing a decision-mode, or a combination of decision-modes (you alone, you with the group, the group alone) to be used in the task of planning the course programme.

2. Using decision-modes in planning. This is the level of planning the course programme. It means working out the details of the programme, making a plan through the use of the decision-modes chosen in 1. This plan will include, in greater or lesser detail, the choice of decision-modes to be used in learning topics within the programme.

3. Using decision-modes in learning. This is the level of learning items within the programme. It means implementing the plan, managing the day-to-day learning activities, using the decision-modes arrived at in 2.

Note that at each level a different decision-mode can be used. As facilitator, you can decide directively (level 1) to plan the course programme by negotiating with group members (level 2); and this plan may delegate some learning activities to be self-managed within the group (level 3). Of course, levels 2 and 3 may each combine decision-modes in different ways.

Figure 3.4 is a diagram to show the fundamental anatomy of power and control options for you, the facilitator, and the group. On this, I call the hierarchical decision-mode, where you alone decide for the group, *direction*; the co-operative, where you decide with the team, *negotiation*; and the autonomous, where you give space to the team to decide by and for itself, *delegation*.

	LEVEL 1 Decision-mode used for choosing ...	**LEVEL 2** decision-modes used in planning, which includes a choice of...	**LEVEL 3** decision-modes used in learning
Hierarchy	*Direction*	*Direction*	*Direction*
Co-operation	*Negotiation*	*Negotiation*	*Negotiation*
Autonomy	*Delegation*	*Delegation*	*Delegation*

Figure 3.4 *The use of decision-modes on three levels*

There are 27 ways you can move across this diagram, combining one entry from each column: 27 basic forms of power and control for facilitator and group. Take an unusual combination, proceeding from left to right: delegation-negotiation-direction. This means that you have delegated to group members the decision about what decision-mode to use in planning, say, the course programme. They have chosen to negotiate the planning with you. And part of that negotiated plan is that you will be making decisions directively in managing the learning activities.

A more conventional combination is the reverse one of direction-negotiation-delegation. Here you have decided on your own, unilaterally, to negotiate with group members in planning the course programme. And the negotiated plan delegates to group members self-directed management of their learning activities. It is essential for any facilitator to get command of this basic diagram, and to be able to reflect on the 27 forms of power.

But of course while the above diagram brings out the basic anatomy of power, it also simplifies the options a great deal. For many combinations of decision-modes may be used within columns 2 and 3, that is, in planning different parts of the course programme, and in different areas of learning activity.

Apollonian and Dionysian planning

By Apollonian planning, I mean the kind of planning implied so far in this chapter: the detailed structuring of future time with topics, resources and methods. Such planning creates a well-defined, temporal map of the course.

It may cover different periods. If the course is for one year with three terms, then a long-range plan covers the whole year, a medium-range plan one term, and a short-range plan one week.

Dionysian planning, by contrast, is impromptu, often improvisatory, responding flexibly and imaginatively to the presence of the group, to its feel and mood and thrust, as well as to the purpose of the course. The Dionysian plan unfolds itself step by step, from one learning activity to the next; and each activity can be chosen by a different decision-mode and executed by a different decision-mode.

So you directively choose one activity, which is managed autonomously by the group; then by negotiation you and the group choose the next activitiy, which is managed by you directively; and so on. Dionysian planning gives you maximum scope for weaving a creative path around the decision-levels table (figure 3.4 above), choosing decision-modes at each level as these seem to be appropriate for the unfolding dynamic of the group.

The Dionysian planner will certainly have the overall objectives in mind; will have a thorough mental grasp of the range of relevant topics, methods and resources; and will probably have a variety of alternative programme outlines in mind. But the actual plan emerges, unfolds, one activity at a time, as the realities of the developing situation make one option feel more fitting than another for the next step.

Some facilitators go through three stages. At the start of their career, when insecure, they create and implement complete Apollonian plans. As their experience, skill and confidence build, they continue to make Apollonian plans, but use them as guidelines only, feeling free to rearrange the schedule in the light of the developing dynamic of the group. In the fully mature stage, they come to the group pregnant with all the possibilities and options, each successive activity being born in the Dionysian mode.

Apollonian planning is good for in-service further training groups, based at the outset on consultation and negotiation, and where there is a good deal of job-relevant subject-matter to be covered. What such a plan lacks in flexibility can be compensated for by blocking in only a very broad outline long-range, and making the detail short- to medium-range, with further planning when the detailed part is covered.

Dionysian planning is good for special skills-building where there is a strong emotional and personal growth dimension, such as co-counselling training for beginners. It gives scope for charismatic command of the group dynamic by the facilitator, giving a secure framework within which beginners can be guided into self-directed catharsis. For non-beginners, a much more consultative Apollonian framework will be appropriate.

The two kinds of planning can be combined in different ways. Thus an Apollonian plan can include longer or shorter periods blocked in for Dionysian planning to be done either by direction, negotiation or by delegation. The Dionysian facilitator can at a certain point in the course break out into the Apollonian mode. There is plenty of scope for interweaving the two.

A decision-mode and a decision-procedure

It is important not to confuse a decision-mode with a decision-procedure. The former refers to the way you, the facilitator, use your power: do you decide for the group, or with the group, or delegate the decision to the group? These are the three decision-modes of hierarchy, co-operation and autonomy. A decision-procedure is a method used for making a collective, group decision: the decision is based on unanimity, or some form of majority vote, or consensus, or gathering the sense of the meeting. I say more about these different decision-procedures later in this chapter in the section on co-operative interventions.

If your decision-mode is hierarchical, i.e. you are being directive, you will not use decision-procedures at all. If you are in the co-operative mode, making some decisions with group members, you and they will use a decision-procedure. And if in the autonomous mode you have delegated some decisions to group members, they on their own will use a decision-procedure.

Six basic decision-modes: an overview

If you examine all the interventions given in the rest of this chapter, you will find that there are six basic decision-modes at the level of programme planning. I present them here as a convenient overview - to provide orientation and perspective. There are two versions of each main mode:

Hierarchical mode

1. Autocratic direction. You decide on the programme without consulting group members, although you may gather relevant information from them.

2. Consultative direction. You decide on the plan after you have gathered in the proposals, evaluations and opinions of group members. The final decision is yours: it may or may not take into account the suggestions you have heard.

Co-operative mode

3. Negotiation. You bring your strong facilitative concerns to the negotiating table and decide on the plan conjointly with the group, seeking agreement, and, where necessary, compromise.

4. Co-ordination. You act as chairperson to the group planning meeting, prompting, guiding and helping the group to make a collective plan. You are not negotiating a plan with the group, but facilitating its emergence - under your touch - from the group. This is more group-centred than negotiation.

Autonomous mode

5. Functional delegation. Either by direction or by negotiation, you delegate to individual members different planning functions, and to the group as a whole a procedure for integrating these strands into a collective plan.

6. Contractual delegation. Within the broad terms of a contract (outlined in terms of time-span and main objectives) determined either by direction or negotiation, you delegate all detailed planning to group members, to manage in their own way.

Note: delegation is necessarily set within limits determined by either direction or negotiation. Absolute delegation means that the facilitator has abandoned his role: the group has become a small political autonomy.

Sometimes, of course, the group will not have power delegated to it, but will seize its autonomy. Either the group is ready for this autonomy, that is, sufficently skilled and aware, or it is not ready, still unskilled and unaware. And either the group wants to exercise this autonomy in a good direction (as you see it), or in a bad direction.

So there are four possibilities: the group is ready for a good goal, unready for a good goal, ready for a bad goal, and unready for a bad goal. The third one of these is unlikely: a skilled and aware group is not likely to want to go in a bad direction - but it is still a possibility. You, the facilitator, should rapidly support the first of these four, strongly confront the relevant parts of the

	Apollonian ⟶ Dionysian		
	LEVEL 1 D-mode for choosing...	**LEVEL 2** a d-mode for planning...	**LEVEL 3** a d-mode for learning
Autocratic direction			
Consultative direction			
Negotiation			
Co-ordination			
Functional delegation			
Contractual delegation			

Figure 3.5 *Apollonian and Dionysian use of decision-levels and decision-modes*

other three, and if the group insists on going ahead, let them do so, but then move in to sort out the confusion when the trial exposes the error.

Figure 3.5 relates the six decision-modes given above to the three levels of decision-making, and to the Apollonian and Dionysian sorts of planning. This is a sophisticated diagram, but it repays meditation on it.

The planning dimension: hierarchical mode

You here choose *for* the group: you direct the planning of the group's learning, deciding unilaterally on the content of the programme, in whole or in part, making decisions for the leaners. For convenience and general relevance, I will take it that you are busy with *planning the course programme*, rather than the whole educational process - although the same interventions apply on the wider scale. And remember, each item can be either *Apollonian* or *Dionysian*.

1. Total directive planning. You are a complete hierarch, planning all aspects of the course programme - topics, time, resources, methods - by yourself, using either 3 or 4, below. But your programme may provide for all three decision-modes - direction, negotiation and delegation - to be used in supervising the planned learning activities. If Dionysian, your planning will be piecemeal and episodic; if Apollonian, it will apply to longer periods.

2. Partial directive planning. You are a hierarch only when planning some aspects of the course programme, using 3 or 4 below; other aspects you plan through negotiation or by delegation. So you are involved in some selection within all three rows of figure 3.6. See also figure 3.3.

	Topics	Time	Resources	Methods
Hierarchy: direction	*Total directive planning stays in this row*			
Co-operation: negotiation	*Partial directive planning adds items from these two rows*			
Autonomy: delegation				

Figure 3.6 *Total and partial directive planning*

3. Autocratic directive planning. You make your planning decisions without consulting group members about their ideas beforehand: you do *not* first seek their proposals and their evaluations of your ideas. You may, however, seek relevant *information only* from the group prior to devising your plan. This is the sort of information needed for you to make sound decisions. For example you might ask each member to give you a list of personal learning needs and goals.

Without rationale. You present your plan without giving any supporting reasons for it, and its advantages over other alternatives.

With rationale. You present your plan and give supporting reasons and stress its advantages.

4. Consultative directive planning. You make your planning decisions after you have consulted the group members who will be affected by them. You gather in their programme proposals and opinions. Lists of individual learning needs are pooled and used by group members to come up with their own timetable design. You genuinely consider these views, but the final version of the plan is yours - it may or may not take into account what group members have suggested.

Facilitator-centred. You disclose in full your provisional plan before you elicit the group's views, which will include evaluations of your proposals and alternative timetable designs. You make a decision on the final plan after considering reactions to your ideas.

Group-centred. You elicit the group members' programme proposals, after stating the broad area for planning, before putting forward your own proposals in full; then make your final version of the plan. This is useful if you want to get a full range of views which are not constrained by any prior statement of yours.

There is a clear distinction between *consultative direction* and *negotiation* and it is important. The former is hierarchical: you retain the right to regard or disregard the views you have elicited from group members, making up your own mind finally. The latter is co-operative: you commit yourself to take into account the views of the group, and to work out an agreed decision with them.

5. Directive planning review and control. You set your criteria for success in implementing your plan, gather in data in the light of these criteria, evaluate the success, and modify the plan or its implementation accordingly. You do all this directively: group members only provide relevant data.

6. Decision-mode directive choice. We shift here to the top level of the three levels of decision-making: the level of choosing the decision-mode to be used in planning. So really this intervention comes first, before 1 to 5 above. It is illustrated in figure 3.7, below. You decide directively, for the group, what sort of decision-mode you are going to use when planning the work programme.

This directive choice may be either autocratic or consultative; but the decision-mode it chooses is not up for negotiation. More than one decision-mode may be selected for different aspects of planning.

At this level you can also choose *directively* a co-operative or autonomous decision-mode for doing the review of planning given in its hierarchical form in 5, above.

	LEVEL 1 D-mode for choosing	LEVEL 2 a d-mode for planning	LEVEL 3 a d-mode for learning
Autocratic direction	*Decision-mode directive choice is in one of these two spaces*		
Consultative direction			
Negotiation		*The choice made will be in one or more of these six spaces*	
Co-ordination			
Functional delegation			
Contractual delegation			
Hierarchical choice by autocratic direction or consultative direction of which decision-modes - direction, negotiation/co-ordination, delegation - to use in planning the course programme - which interrelates topics, time, resources and methods. Methods will include decision-modes to be used in the learning activities.			

Figure 3.7 *Decision-mode directive choice*

7. Decision-mode mastery. The above model can now be extended to give you comprehensive mental mastery of the power-structure involved in facilitating an experiential learning group. First a reminder of the three different levels at which decision-modes can be applied.

Level 1. Using a decision-mode to choose a decision-mode to be used in planning the programme.

Level 2. Using a decision-mode in the planning of the programme. This will include choosing decision-modes to be used in learning activities.

Level 3. Using a decision-mode in managing the learning activities. When the group members are busy with some exercise, are you directing them, or collaborating with them, or are they managing it on their own?

These levels and the full range of choices that can be made are shown in figure 3.8. So a tick in the third box down in the first column means that you have elected to negotiate with group members about which decision-modes to use for planning the course programme. If there are also ticks in the third and sixth boxes in the second column, this means that your negotiation with the group at level 1 resulted in an agreement that some part of the planning would be negotiated with you, and the rest would be delegated to group members. And if, finally, there are also ticks in the bottom two boxes of the third column, this means that the programme resulting from both the negotiated and the delegated planning includes only the use of delegation in the management of all learning activities.

	LEVEL 1 D-mode for choosing	LEVEL 2 a d-mode for planning	LEVEL 3 a d-mode for learning
Autocratic direction			
Consultative direction			
Negotiation	*You use one or more modes in this column to select...*	*the use of one or more modes in this column for making a plan which will include a selection for...*	*the use of one or more modes in this column for managing the different learning activities*
Co-ordination			
Functional delegation			
Contractual delegation			

You use one or more modes in level 1 to choose one or more modes in level 2 for use in planning the course programme - which interrelates topics, time, resources and methods. The planning of methods will include one or more decision-modes to be used in level 3 in managing the various learning activities.

Figure 3.8 *Decision-mode mastery*

Figure 3.8 goes beyond the hierarchical mode - which is the focus of this section of the chapter - since it includes co-operative and autonomous decision-modes. But you have not really mastered the hierarchical mode of planning, if you have not also mastered this wider context of options within which it is set.

It will take a good hierarch to help a group master and put to good use the subtleties and complexities of the power-structure which this table lays bare.

The planning dimension: co-operative mode

You plan the course programme, in whole or in part, *with* the group. You are committed to negotiate, to take into account and seek agreement with the views of group members in constructing the timetable. Decisions are collaborative; you have abandoned any right to final unilateral control. But you press strongly the claims of your own point of view. Where you and the group differ strongly, you seek compromise rather than unilateral surrender.

There is, however, an important difference between *negotiating* with the group and *co-ordinating* the group, i.e. chairing a group planning meeting. In the former you represent you educational values and concerns, and request that the group come to terms with them, although you never impose them. The latter is more group-centred, and your profile is lower: power shifts over to the collective, on which you discreetly exercise your influence through the chair and your vote. Both are clearly in the co-operative mode.

There is another important difference, already discussed on page 48, between a decision-mode and a decision-procedure. By a *decision-mode* I mean whether the facilitator is exercising power in the hierarchical, co-operative or autonomous modes - that is, by direction, negotiation or delegation. By a *decision-procedure* I mean the way in which a collective decision is made - by the group as a whole - by voting, or other examples I give below. It applies only in the co-operative and autonomous modes.

So co-operative decision-modes can now be used in five ways, which can be described in the context of the three levels of decision-making which I introduced on page 45.

Level 1. Co-operative choice of a decision-mode to use in planning.

Level 2. Co-operative planning of the course programme.

Level 2a. Co-operative choice of a decision-procedure to be used in cooperative planning.

Level 3. Co-operative management of a learning activity.

Level 3a. Co-operative choice of a decision-procedure to be used in the co-operative management of a learning activity.

1. Total co-operative planning. All the major aspects of planning are agreed between you and the group and all major programme decisions reached by conjoint negotiation or co-ordination. A programme entirely decided by

	Topics	Time	Resources	Methods
Co-operation: *negotiation*	*Total co-operative planning stays in this row*			
Hierarchy: *direction*	*Partial co-operative planning adds items from these two rows*			
Autonomy: *delegation*				

Figure 3.9 *Total and partial co-operative planning*

negotiation may, in its choice of learning methods, include all the decision-modes for managing different kinds of learning activity.

2. Partial co-operative planning. Only some aspects of planning are decided by conjoint negotiation or co-ordination. Others are decided by direction or delegation: you are involved in some selection within all three rows shown in figure 3.9.

3. Facilitator-centred negotiated planning. This creates a *group learning contract*. You first propose your version of the course programme, then invite group members to propose their modifications of it, and negotiate with them until the final version is agreed. This can be preceded by people writing out lists of personal learning needs. It is best to reach a decision by a *consensus* decision-procedure, as defined in 9 below.

Strong form. You present a fully detailed programme for the group to consider and negotiate on.

Weak form. You give only broad outlines of a programme, modify and agree on this, then work with the group to fill it in. This is close to 4, next.

4. Group-centred negotiated planning. This also creates a *group learning contract*. You first invite group members to propose their version of a course programme, then propose your modifications of it, and negotiate with them until a final version is agreed. This can be preceded by people writing out lists of personal learning needs. It is best to reach a decision by a *consensus* decision-procedure, as defined in 9 below.

Strong form. You ask the group to present a fully finished programme for negotiation.

Weak form. You ask the group for a broad outline only, which you then work on together with them.

5. Group-centred co-ordinated planning. This is a third approach to making a *group learning contract*. You are not negotiating a course programme with group members, but simply co-ordinate their decision-making. You will need to agree some form of decision-procedure, as in 9 below. You act as chairperson to group members' planning meetings, helping them clarify their final version of a programme. As chairperson, you are still influential, raising task and process issues for the group to consider: you have a voice and a vote. This is still more group-centred than group-centred negotiation. It is close to the autonomous mode.

6. One-to-one negotiated planning. You and one group member negotiate an *individual learning contract* over a specified time for that person. The negotiation can be facilitator-centred or member-centred, as in 3 and 4 above. The plan includes an interim review of progress with possible modification of the contract in the light of this, and review at the end of the specified time regarding the degree of success in implementing the contract.

Note. Remember that any learning contract, whether group or individual, may include within it all the decision-modes, applied to the management of different kinds of learning activity. So it can be agreed in the contract that some learning activity is directed by you, some is in collaboration with you, and some is self- or peer directed and autonomous.

7. Co-operative programme review and control. You agree with the group on a set of criteria for success in implementing a group learning contract, and on ways of gathering in relevant data. You may use collaborative assessment: see Chapter 4, item 13, the meaning dimension, co-operative mode, page 72. After some period of implementation, you together consider the data and seek a consensus evaluation. As a result you may renegotiate the contract, and make agreed changes in it or look at learning performance and effectiveness. This is collaborative monitoring of learning after collaborative planning of it. Of course, you could also have collaborative review after directive, or autonomous, planning.

8. Open door negotiation and renegotiation. You are available on an *ad hoc* basis to negotiate filling gaps in the original programme, impromptu plans for new times, and to renegotiate old plans not suited to members' goals and needs.

9. Decision-procedure negotiation. You seek agreement with the group on how to reach a final decision, for example in 5, group-centred co-ordinated planning. First of all, the group will need to understand the range of decision-procedures:

Unanimous vote. A decision is reached when everyone votes in favour.

Percentage majority vote. A decision is reached when the majority vote reaches a certain percentage of those voting.

Simple majority vote. A decision is reached when the majority vote is over a half of those voting.

Consensus. The most *acceptable* solution for all. A decision is reached when the minority agrees that its views have been heard and understood and yet still rejected; and when it assents to abide by the majority view it dislikes the least.

Gathering the sense of the meeting. There is no formal vote. After a full airing of views, the chairperson gathers the sense of the meeting into a proposed decision. If there is dissent from this proposal, the discussion continues. The chairperson then gathers the sense of the meeting into a second proposal. This process continues until the gathered sense is assented to. Someone else may gather the sense of the meeting, and put it to the chair; especially if the sense is eluding the chairperson.

You and the group will have to use a decision-procedure in deciding which decision-procedure to choose for use in co-operative planning. You just have to go for one in order to avoid the lurking infinite regress of deciding which one to use in deciding which one to use etc.

All these decision-procedures presuppose that they have been preceded by some good discussion-procedure, which ensures that everyone has a say, that no-one overtalks and dominates and that no clique railroads through its views. An obvious rule is that no-one speaks twice until everyone has spoken once, and then perhaps no-one thrice until everyone twice.

10. Decision-procedure review and renegotiation. After a period of using an agreed decision-procedure, you review its use with the group, and renegotiate to continue its use or to change to some other procedure.

11. Decision-mode co-operative choice. We again shift here to the top level of the three levels of decision-making, as in 6 under the hierarchical mode: the level of choosing the decision-mode to be used in planning. So really this intervention comes first, before all the ones above. See figure 3.10 below.

	LEVEL 1 D-mode for choosing	LEVEL 2 a d-mode for planning	LEVEL 3 a d-mode for learning
Autocratic direction			
Consultative direction			
Negotiation	*Decision-mode co-operative choice*	*The choice made will be in one*	
Co-ordination	*is in one of these two spaces*	*or more of these six spaces*	
Functional delegation			
Contractual delegation			
Co-operative choice by negotiation or co-ordination of which decision-modes - direction, negotiation/co-ordination, delegation - to use in planning the course programme - which interrelates topics, time, resources and methods. Methods will include decision-modes to be used in the learning activities.			

Figure 3.10 *Decision-mode co-operative choice*

You decide by negotiating with the group, what sort of decision-mode you are going to use when planning the course programme. This negotiation may be *facilitator-centred*, in which you press the claims for some decision-mode first; or it may be *group-centred*, where you ask the group members to put forward their case for a decision-mode before you do. You present the range of decision-modes - autocratic or consultative direction, negotiation, co-ordination and the two forms of delegation - and negotiate with the team which one or more of them to use in planning the course programme.

12. Decision-mode review and renegotiation. You invite the whole group to review with you the effectiveness of some decision-mode that is currently in use for planning. This may lead on to renegotiating the mode. Or the review may take place after the planning is over, and so may influence the choice of decision-mode for future planning.

13. Renegotiation clause. You encourage shared leadership by building in a collaboration clause from the start of the group. This clause states: 'It is in principle open to anyone at any time to seek to negotiate any change in the learning programme, and to ask for an appropriate time to conduct this negotiation.' Of course, this clause is given scope in a co-operative review as in 7 above. Equally, the clause may empower someone to call for such a review.

The planning dimension: autonomous mode

Here you are getting out of the way, affirming the group's need to do its own planning and to sort out issues of power and control in deciding what to do. You delegate the planning of the course programme, in whole or in part, to the group. The decision to delegate some planning to the group is, of course, made at decision-level 1, and could be made directively by you, or by negotiation with the group, or by the group through delegation at level 1.

Sometimes, to repeat the important point made earlier in this chapter, the group will not have planning delegated to it, but will appropriate its autonomy. Either it makes a mature claim for independence, rooted in skill and knowledge; or it tries to seize its power when it is not ripe enough. It is wise to support and encourage the former, and resist and confront the latter. However, if group members insist in going ahead with their premature seizure of power, let them do so, and later you can help to sort out the confusion when the trial exposes the error.

Another point is that you can delegate a chunk of planning to the group as a whole, and let the members sort out who does what, and how they work together. This I call *contractual delegation*. Or you can delegate particular planning functions to individuals and also a procedure whereby they can readily integrate their strands into a collective plan. This I call *functional delegation*. I discuss these two below.

A special case of delegation is in a training the trainers' group, where you delegate your own role to one person in the group for them to practise being a facilitator of course design. So their task is to manage a part of real planning of the training that is to take place in the group. Your delegation can say what decision-mode to use, or not.

1. Total delegated planning. All aspects of programme planning are decided autonomously by group members, using 3 or 5 below. You play no part in the process. You become redundant as a facilitator in the planning stage. The group becomes an autonomy, a totally self-directed peer planning group. If the plan itself excludes your having any facilitative role in the learning activities, then you have been given the boot, and your career with this group is over. However, the plan may programme you to facilitate some of the learning activities using the decision-modes of direction or negotiation. But you can't do any of this unless you agree to it, so negotiation, if only tacit, comes back in here.

2. Partial delegated planning. You arrange that only some aspects of course planning are delegated for the group to decide, using 3 or 5 below, while others are done by direction or negotiation. 1 and 2 are shown in figure 3.11.

	Topics	Time	Resources	Methods
Autonomy: *delegation*	*Total delegated planning stays in this row*			
Hierarchy: *direction*	*Partial delegated planning adds items from these two rows*			
Co-operation: *negotiation*				

Figure 3.11 *Total and partial delegated planning*

3. Contractually delegated group planning. You define with the group, by direction or negotiation, a whole block of learning in terms of its main objectives and the overall time to be taken for it; or in terms of some other broad parameters. Within this outline contract, all planning is undertaken by group members on their own: they decide who does what and how they work together. This is the *autonomous peer group learning contract*.

4. Contractually delegated individual planning. Here you define with one individual, by direction or negotiation, a whole block of learning in terms of its main objectives and the overall time to be taken for it; or in terms of some other broad parameters. Within this outline contract, all planning is undertaken by the individual alone, in their own way. This is the *autonomous individual learning contract*.

5. Functionally delegated group planning. By direction or negotiation, you delegate to different individuals in the group different planning functions, i.e. responsibility for planning different aspects of the course programme. And to the whole group you delegate an integrating procedure whereby it can bring these strands together and plan collectively. There will have to be some outline contract about overall time and range of learning; so this item puts more structure into 3, above. This is the *semi-autonomous peer group learning contract*.

6. Functionally delegated individual planning. By direction or negotiation, you delegate to one individual responsibility for planning a personal learning programme. You also delegate a procedure for effective planning which that person can follow. There will have to be some outline contract about overall time and range of learning; so this item puts more structure into 4, above. This is the *semi-autonomous individual learning contract*.

7. Autonomous programme review and control. Part of what is delegated in 3, 4, 5 and 6, is a commitment to hold an autonomous interim review of the contract in the light of implementing some of it, leading to possible revision of the contract, or more control over pacing the learning. Of course, this review could go back into the collaborative mode, and involve you, the facilitator.

8. Trainee-trainer delegation. You delegate your own role to one group member, to practise facilitation on some real chunk of programme planning that is needed for the current group - which, of course, will be a training the trainers' group. You may specify in the delegation what decision-mode the trainee is to use in facilitating the planning; or you may leave it to the trainee's own judgment. Remember you can also delegate to someone the practice of Dionysian planning. A more limited kind of trainee-trainer delegation is to ask someone to take over facilitating the selection and use of some decision-procedure to co-ordinate group planning.

9. Planning initiative clause. You have delegated to group members the right to take unilateral initiatives - changing the existing programme and creating contingency plans - as emerging learning needs and interests require. This clause may be attached to a plan made by any decision-mode. It may pervade the whole ethos of the team as a form of self-directing facilitation.

10. Autonomous participation clause. You affirm at the outset of the group, with occasional reminders if necessary, a strong participants' autonomy clause. This states:

> 'Whenever I or anyone else proposes an activity, please feel free to participate or not participate in it, according to your own judgment about whether it seems relevant and appropriate to your own needs and interests. You are under no pressure from me and hopefully no-one else in the group to engage in any activity which you do not freely choose. Your right to abstain from participation will be fully respected.'

When a member double-binds about joining in some activity, that is, appears to be saying both yes and no in different verbal and non-verbal ways, then you can confront the person until an unequivocal choice is made. If the choice is finally no, then you instantly accept and respect this. No-one should be *constrained* to engage in any activity to enhance their growth.

An autonomy clause, clearly stated in principle, and fully honoured in practice, is in my view an essential moral component of an experiential learning group. It is also psychologically effective: when members really feel they can say no, they discover a more powerful motivation within to say yes. Persons are only fully respected when, among other things, they have the right to dissociate. If the dissociation is purely defensive, rooted in avoidance, persons still have the right to hold on to their defences as long they choose. And again, saying a fully defensive no, loud and clear, often creates the space for saying a risk-taking yes at a later date.

11. Dionysian autonomy phase. If you are busy with Dionysian, step-by-step planning, one activity generating the next, then for a certain length of time you make no planning interventions of any sort about what the group is going to do. Nor do you facilitate the choice of decision-modes and decision-procedures. No prompts, no guidance, no reminders or consciousness-raising: you keep entirely silent about planning and decision levels. You announce the start of an autonomy phase, and explain its rationale: a time for the group to practise autonomous Dionysian planning - or to go Apollonian if they wish. This strategy still allows you to make interventions on the other dimensions.

12. Going out. One dramatic way of underlining any kind of autonomous planning in the group, is for you to go out of the room when it is going on. This has the advantage of preventing the group from trying to fall back on your resources, or being dependently distracted by your presence. The disadvantage is that you get no insight into difficulties encountered.

13. Autonomy lab. This overlaps with the strategy of autonomous structuring of a group's learning experience (see 12, the structuring dimension, autonomous mode, page 125). A whole workshop, or major part of a workshop, is devoted to this strategy. You are only a resource, alongside all other resources (books, tapes, TV, etc.), and only do anything when asked by participants to meet some specific learning need (Harrison, 1973).

Group members exercise total initiative and autonomy in deciding what their learning needs are, how to meet them, in what order and with whom. *All* planning is self- or peer directed, and you are not involved in it at any point. It is also entirely Dionysian and multiple, with many different short-term plans emerging alongside each other all round the room.

The planning sequence is: first autonomous decision-making by each participant about personal learning needs, how to meet them and in what order, then some co-operative decision-making with others with similar learning needs, then maybe an approach to you to do some work to meet those needs.

Of course, in an autonomy lab, you may never be approached at all. In which case, you can enter the peer group, and set about meeting your own learning needs, taking initiatives, co-operating with others, and so on. There has to be a proviso here, that you will give up doing your own thing, if some person or small group want to call upon you as a resource.

However, you are not the only, or even the primary, resource. The point about an autonomy lab is that it is a peer teaching as well as a peer learning situation. Everyone is a potential resource for everyone else. Thus at the outset each person needs to identify what knowledge, skills and experience they have to offer, as well as what it is they want to learn.

This is one of the most profitable kinds of learning experience. It is the most total form of delegation on the part of you, the facilitator. Once done, autonomy becomes the primary value, and you function as a facilitator only under contract to autonomous learners - a contract which they initiate and define.

14. Planning to transfer the learning. Group members take time, in pairs or small groups, to support each other in setting up goals and making action-plans that will transfer what they have learned within the group to their work and personal life outside the group. This can be made a regular feature of long-term day-release courses, with each person reporting back to their support group on how the transfer went.

15. Claiming power. This, of course, is not an intervention of yours, but it requires a response. The group want to take over the planning and do it independently, either before you have made any proposals about the matter, or after you have decided on a hierarchical or co-operative mode of planning. As I wrote in the introduction to this section on the autonomous mode, either the group makes a mature claim for independence, rooted in skill and knowledge, or it tries to seize its power when it is not ripe enough. It is wise to support and encourage the former, and resist and confront the latter. However, if group members insist in going ahead with their premature seizure of power, let them do so, and later you can help to sort out the confusion when the trial exposes the error.

4. The meaning dimension

This dimension is concerned with giving meaning to the experiences which group members are having - individually, in particular interactions, in small group learning activities and in the group as a whole. Your concern here is with how the participants make sense of what is happening and acquire understanding.

Four forms of understanding

Understanding is the core of learning. To learn something is to understand it and to retain that understanding. If the focus is all on retention and with little understanding, then we get mere rote learning, or learning by heart. If the focus is all on understanding with no retention, we get flashes of insight which fade as soon as they light up and have no power to kindle future thought or behaviour. To learn properly is to understand and to rehearse that understanding, take charge of it, so that it becomes influential from its base in the memory.

As with learning, there are four kinds of understanding. I state them in a learning cycle sequence, as distinct from the epistemological hierarchy of the four kinds of learning given in Chapter 1 (see Chapter 8, Figure 8.3, page 127, showing the learning cycle and the hierarchy together).

1. Conceptual understanding. This is understanding that something is the case, evident in and expressed in statements and propositions.

2. Imaginal understanding. This is understanding configurations in form and process, evident in and expressed in the symbolism of line, shape, colour, proportion, sequence, sound, rhythm, movement.

3. Practical understanding. This is understanding how to act, how to do something, evident in and expressed in some practical skill.

4. Experiential understanding. This is understanding by encounter, by direct acquaintance, by entering *into* some state of being. It is manifest through the process of being there, face-to-face with the person, at the event, in the experience.

I use the term *experiential learning* as a shorthand for the process of interweaving these four sorts of understanding in such a way that they make a relatively permanent change in a person's behaviour and state of being.

Imaginal understanding is often neglected in accounts of the learning process, yet it is clearly central in, for example, mediating between conceptual understanding and practical understanding. If someone explains to me in conceptual terms what to do in order to swing a golf club correctly, I have intuitively to convert this into an imaginal understanding of the whole configuration of stance and movement involved, as a basis for building up my practical skill.

The experiential learning cycle

The basic form of interweaving the four kinds of understanding is the experiential learning cycle. Suppose the group is learning some interpersonal skill. The trainees start with some *conceptual understanding,* listening to the trainer make descriptive statements about what is involved in exercising this skill. They then move to *imaginal understanding,* forming a rough image of the form and sequence of behaviours that manifest the skill. This guides them in practising the skill, where they start to get *practical understanding* of how to do it. Practice brings the skill into relation with another person; and so they enter into an *experiential understanding* of the dynamic encounter with the other. Practising the skill interacts with the dynamic of the encounter: practical and experiential understanding continuously modify each other.

Then there is feedback on the practice, which starts the second cycle. Feedback returns them to conceptual understanding: it reflects on what went on in the practical and experiential phases of understanding, seeking to spotlight it through the use of words and concepts. It applies standards, picking out good and bad practice. This leads to a revised and enriched imaginal understanding, a better image of the form and sequence of behaviours; thence to better practice, and so on. Figure 4.1 maps out the cycles:

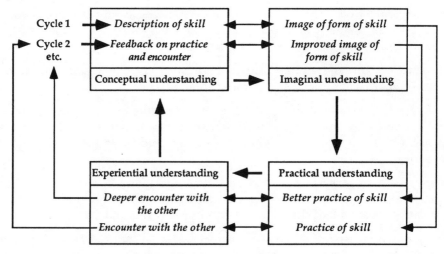

Figure 4.1 *The experiential learning cycle*

The upper level of the diagram represents the reflection phase, where thinking and imagination interact (shown by the two-way arrows); the lower level represents the action phase, where there is an interplay between one's behaviour and encounter with the other (shown by the two-way arrows). While the main thrust of the cycle is clear, the four kinds of learning are much more involved in each other at each stage than the diagram can show. Going round the cycle several times enhances learning, as each kind of understanding successively clarifies every other kind.

There is also a complementary form of the experiential learning cycle, which starts with practice at the bottom right-hand corner. After a phase of practice and encounter, the learner steps back to conceptualize what went on and to evolve a model of good practice, imagines the whole form of this model, takes it back into better practice and so on.

The experiential learning cycle, in either form, is either used explicitly and formally in structured exercises; or in the broader sweep of the group's development as it moves between phases of active learning and times for review of what it is about. In advanced stages of learning, it can be developed into full-blown co-operative inquiry - see 15 under the co-operative mode, page 73.

When the cycle is used within a structured exercise for interpersonal skills training, then you do the conceptual modelling of the skill at the start of the cycle. The trainees discuss the model with you and build up their imaginal grasp of it. The trainees are on their own in the practical and experiential phases, and also when they return to the conceptual level of feedback and reflection on practice, which takes place in the small practice sub-group. The feedback and reflection can be continued in the large group, with sharing between sub-groups, and involving you in the general review. What is learnt from this review is then taken back into practice to improve performance, and so on. This sequence is examined in detail in Chapter 7.

From the point of view of the decision-modes, first you are hierarchical in modelling, then they are autonomous in practice, experience, feedback and reflection, then you co-operate with them in a general review, then they are autonomous again in practice, and so on.

Areas of understanding

Understanding can be applied in three main areas, which are understanding the task, understanding the group process, and understanding the learning process itself. The task may mean some subject matter, an interpersonal skill, a piece of personal growth work, or whatever. Group process refers to what is going on within and between people, where this is not itself part of the task. The third of these means understanding what is involved in getting to understand the task or the process: upper-level learning about ground-floor learning. If we put the four forms of understanding with the three areas, we get the table shown in figure 4.2, below. It provides a map of 12 different ways in which participants in an experiential learning group can make sense of what is going on.

	Task	Group process	Learning process
Conceptual understanding			
Imaginal understanding			
Practical understanding			
Experiential understanding			

Figure 4.2 *Forms and areas of understanding*

Most of the interventions below relate to conceptual understanding and to imaginal understanding in one or other of the three areas. The occasion of their use will be in the feedback and reflection phases of a structured exercise using the experiential learning cycle, or in reflective episodes about the whole development of learning in the group.

Practical and experiential understanding come under the structuring of learning activities, which is the subject of Chapter 7.

The meaning dimension: hierarchical mode

The basic strategy here is for you to make sense of what is going on *for* the group, or one or more persons in it. You give meaning to events, illuminate them, either by taking time out to provide some general, theoretical rationale of group dynamics and experiential learning, or by making a particular interpretation of some episode, in the midst of it or just after it, or by some form of demonstration or presentation.

You may be expounding some subject matter relevant to a task, or giving feedback on the execution of a task. You may do all this in the *imaginal* as well as in the *conceptual* way.

After you give your interpretation or information, whether to the whole group or to one or two people only, you have a choice. You can continue to be the hierarch, and leave it there to hover and make its impact, without any follow-up; or you can shift over into the co-operative mode and elicit reactions, views and comments, alternative perspectives - and work *with* the group in seeking to understand what has gone on.

1. Theoretical input. Your input may present in conceptual form any kind of information relevant to current learning. In a skills training group, the input may give the conceptual background and descriptive modelling of behaviour to be practised in some structured exercise. It is the first phase - conceptual understanding - of the experiential learning cycle.

You may present some theoretical model of what goes on in experiential groups, maybe with some of the research findings about different aspects of such groups. The model may use group dynamic, psychodynamic, sociodynamic or transpersonal concepts, or some mixture of these. The input may be at the start of the group, during it, or at the end of it. It will be followed by question and answer. The purpose of the input is to provide members with some basic conceptual orientation which they can use to make sense of the group process. It gives a general framework; it isn't aimed at particular persons or particular episodes.

2. Imaginal input. With respect to the task, the group process or the learning process, you seek to evoke *imaginal understanding* through the use of one or more of the following methods.

Metaphor. The imaginative use of myth, metaphor, allegory, fable and story to convey meaning.

Instance. You describe an illustrative incident, or dramatic case study, from real life.

Resonance. You recount associations and memories evoked by what is going on, in order to find meaning through resonance with the form of other situations, which may be from some quite different field.

Presentation. You present non-verbal analogies in the form of graphics, paintings, music or movement.

Dramaturgy. You combine *metaphor* with *presentation* in a creative piece of mime or theatre.

Demonstration. You show in your own behaviour, both verbal and non-verbal, what it is you mean: you model a skill in action, positively showing it well done, and negatively showing how it can degenerate.

Caricature. You give feedback to someone by mimicking their behaviour and caricaturing - in a kind way - the salient features to which you wish to draw their attention.

All this is to help participants get an imaginative grasp of basic configurations of form and process in the area of concern. In a skills training group, any of these methods can be used to help the trainees create an imaginal model of the behaviour that is to be practised.

3. Video shows. You make a direct appeal to imaginal understanding by showing a video that exhibits some behaviour you want to convey. The video demonstrations can use caricature and selective emphasis to get their point across.

4. Handouts. You provide these to back up the sorts of input given in 1, 2 and 3 above. They include all kinds of written material, diagrams and other graphics, reproductions of paintings, music discs, video and audio tapes.

5. Attributive interpretation. You attribute simple psychological meaning to some current piece of behaviour in the group, in terms of intention, motive, desire, wish, emotion, thought, and any other such everyday psychological concepts.

The attribution may be to what is overt in the behaviour, for example to help A notice the behaviour of B - 'A, B has just clearly shown that he wants to get to know you better' - or it may be to what is covert in the behaviour, to help people become more aware of their own process - 'There seems to be a great deal of anger implicit in this exchange of views'. It may be directed at the group as a whole, but is more likely to be aimed at some interactive sub-group, or an individual member.

6. Psychodynamic interpretation. You give meaning to some current episode in the group in psychodynamic terms. It is more theory-laden than a simple attribution. It is always aimed at particular persons and particular behaviour.

> *Present process.* The interpretation deals only with the current state of the psyche in terms of some theoretical model. You may interpret some behaviour in terms, for example, of the Jungian four functions and their current dynamic interaction. You may interpret a defensive form of behaviour only in terms of existential anxiety (see Chapter 2, page 33).

> *Present and past process.* This kind of interpretation identifies current behaviour as a distortion due to unfinished emotional business from the past, with those involved acting out maladaptive survival mechanisms of early life, adopting various defensive behaviours in the group to avoid issues that stir up buried, painful trauma. Here, therefore, you interpret these behaviours in terms of archaic anxiety reinforcing the existential.

7. Sociodynamic interpretation. You give meaning to what is going on in more sociological terms, and seek to raise group consciousness about how decisions are or are not being made; how issues of authority and leadership are shaping events; how tacit norms constrain behaviour; how members attain identity by informal allocation of roles; how contribution rates, hierarchies and pecking orders become established; communication networks; subgroups and conflict; and so on. Again, these interpretations are aimed at specific events and persons.

8. Transcendental interpretation. You make unusual sense of some specific happening in religious and occult terms, by relating it to the movement of the spirit, of divine energy; the influence of the ancestors, spirits, presences; the effect of occult forces or the play of archetypal powers from other dimensions of being; extensions or shifts in experience of space or time; the awakening of *kundalini* in the psychic body; sudden strange episodes of extrasensory perception or psychokinesis; encounter with deeper aspects of human destiny and the human condition; and so on.

This way of making sense of events is more likely to be applied in meditation or enlightenment workshops, and in transpersonal, charismatic, psychic and occult training groups. But there is no reason why it should not be used, with appropriate discretion, in any kind of group. For there are occasions, whatever the agenda, when another reality is present.

9. Imaginal interpretation. Each of the above from 5 to 8 can also be presented in different imaginal forms by using one or more of *metaphor, instance, resonance, presentation, dramaturgy, demonstration* a n d *caricature*, as these are defined in 2, above. This direct appeal to imaginal understanding of *form* can be used alone, or with conceptual interpretation. It can give insight on several levels at once.

10. Conceptual feedback on an exercise. Where structured exercises are being used for skills building or personal growth or anything else, then you give direct descriptive and evaluative feedback to the participant who has just taken a turn. This feedback may overlap with some of the above kinds of interpretation, but will have special reference to the particular purpose of the given exercise. Negative feedback is usefully followed by an immediate rerun of the exercise.

11. Imaginal feedback on an exercise. You can use mimicry and caricature in live demonstration as feedback - showing in your own behaviour how the form of the trainee's action has gone awry. There are all the other imaginal devices of *metaphor, instance, resonance, presentation* and *dramaturgy* as in 2, above.

12. Micro-cue feedback. This is used in structured exercise feedback. It is aimed at the small details of behaviour: a turn of phrase, a tone of voice, an inflection, a gesture, a posture. You make a simple attributive interpretation: stating how each small item reveals a certain state or attitude of mind. You can give imaginal feedback by caricaturing the trainee's micro-cues in your own behaviour.

Micro-cue feedback is very important in the reshaping and fine-tuning of behavioural skills.

13. Facilitator explanation. You explain what you are doing, have done, or are about to do, and why. This can apply at any level: selecting a decision-mode for planning, planning, facilitating some piece of learning.

14. Review of the learning process. You throw light on how the learning is being managed or is proceeding in the group. You can do this by descriptive statements, to aid conceptual understanding, or by the imaginal devices presented in 2, above. As a hierarchical intervention, that is, one that does not lead into a sharing of perspectives within the group, it will probably occur quite early on in a beginners' group.

15. Unilateral assessment. You assess the learning performance of group members, without involving them either in the selection of criteria or the act of assessment. This exclusion of the learner from the process of assessment is educationally unsound, and out of date today. So also is unilateral course evaluation, in which you alone pass judgement on the effectiveness of course design and methods, your own style, and other matters to do with the course as such.

The meaning dimension: co-operative mode

You do not give your meaning to what is going on, but alert members to something that is happening in the group, some aspect of its task or process, and prompt them to seek out and give *their own* meaning to it. You may then add your view, as one idea among others, without necessarily claiming special status for it. You invite group members to participate with you in the generation of understanding. Whether the whole group, a sub-group, or just one person, is the focus, the idea is for you encourage a pooling and sharing of perspectives, including your own.

The first interventions below prompt group members, as something is happening, to give their own interpretation to it. You, therefore, choose the behaviour that is to be interpreted, but invite the group to make the first interpretations. There is a hierarchical element in the choosing and pointing out, but the primary thrust of the intervention and its intent is co-operative. You are seeking to elicit an exchange of ideas between you and the group.

The later interventions enable you to dialogue with the group about autonomous self- and peer determined ideas and evaluations.

1. Invite verbal interpretation. You ask a question which draws attention to something going on and invites someone to make sense of it, to give it a meaning. This question can be nonspecific or quite specific about the happening; and also nonspecific or quite specific about what sort of interpretation is being prompted. If I say 'What is going on in this group right now?', I am being nonspecific about what behaviour I am pointing to, and about what sort of interpretation (attributive, psychodynamic, sociodynamic, transcendental) I am seeking. If I say 'Is our physical behaviour being constrained by some tacit norm?', I am being more specific on both fronts. So there is here a whole spectrum of prompts, from those that are very open-ended to those that are very closed round one piece of behaviour and seek out one precise interpretation.

2. Facilitating self-discovery. Working co-operatively with a group member, picking up on their cues, and prompting with questions as in 1, you invite just one person to make sense of their personal experience. You may complement this by inviting feedback from other group members, and by giving some yourself.

3. Describing behaviour. You simply make a descriptive comment about some observable piece of behaviour, without attaching any kind of interpretation to it, or without asking anyone to interpret it. 'We have been discussing this for an hour'; 'We are all sitting with our arms crossed'; 'Peter, you never look at Jane when you speak to her'. This may, or may not, lead to some airing of views about what the described behaviour signifies. You may or may not join in this; indeed, you may not be sure what meaning, if any, to attach to the observation.

4. Indicating behaviour. This is the same as 3, except that you don't pick out the observed behaviour verbally, but non-verbally, by gesture, touch, the direction of the gaze. This invites imaginal understanding first of all.

5. Invite mythic interpretation. Ask group members to be creative in the use metaphor, allegory, phantasy, fable or story, to give an account of some task or process issue and generate imaginal understanding of it. You join in the sharing and discussion of myths.

6. Invite interpretation by resonance. Invite group members to share any associations and memories evoked by what is going on in the group, in order to find meaning through resonance with the form of other situations. You share you own associations, and join in the general discussion.

7. Invite presentational feedback. You invite one or more group members to give imaginal meaning to what has just been going on, by symbolizing it non-verbally in movement, a group sculpture made out of body postures, vocal sounds or instrumental music, a painting or drawing. You may add your own presentational account.

Feedback on these presentations may then lead over into a sharing of verbal interpretations, including yours; so the group moves from imaginal to conceptual understanding. This may relate to either task or process.

8. Invite dramaturgical feedback. You ask participants to improvise a mime or spoken drama which portrays some current task or process issue.

9. Invite mimicry feedback. Invite one or more group members to mimic and caricature some piece of behaviour that one or two people are busy with, so that there is a variety of imaginal showings of the behaviour. It is essential that mimicry and caricature are benign and not malicious. Join in the general discussion that follows.

10. Further feedback and reflection in the whole group. After self- and peer feedback and reflection within a small group exercise that is using the experiential learning cycle formally (see 1, autonomous mode, page 74), you invite further sharing in the whole group and with you. This yields more learning for the group and gives you the opportunity to discuss issues that arise from the sharing and to negotiate what to sharpen up in the next round of practice.

11. Group process review. You invite the group, every once in a while, to look back on a whole phase of its activity and to identify and evaluate the various aspects of its process. You may prompt by raising different categories and aspects for consideration, including your own facilitator style, its use of dimensions and modes. You may share your own views among views that are put forward by the group and lead into a general discussion on the dynamic of the group. This can be both verbal/conceptual and by all the various imaginal devices given in 2, page 67. Conceptually, the review can be developed into model and theory-building based on the group's own process.

12. Task and learning process review. This item also overlaps with 7, co-operative programme review, planning dimension, co-operative mode, see page 56. Together with the group, you periodically take time out to reflect on what is being learnt, how it is being learnt and whether it is being learnt.

Note. 11 and 12 represent the reflection phase of the experiential learning cycle as applied informally within the whole development of the group.

13. Collaborative assessment. You agree criteria of competence with the group, its members use these for self- and peer assessment, you use them to assess the group members and negotiate a final assessment with them. This is a combination of self-, peer and facilitator assessment of learning performance. You will need to give group members a structure for doing this, and train and supervise them in the early use of it. The basic stages are:

Negotiated criteria-setting. You talk and negotiate with group members until you all agree on a few basic criteria of competence, relevant to the skill being assessed. This is facilitator-centred if you present your criteria first, before negotiation, and group-centred if participants present all their criteria first. For a full discussion, see Heron (1988a).

Self-assessment. Each individual assesses their own competence, in front of their peers and of you, dealing with strengths and weaknesses in the light of each criterion.

Peer assessment. Group members take it in turns to assess - in the light of each criterion - the competence of the person who has just completed their self-assessment, with special reference to overplayed, underplayed or omitted strengths and weaknesses in the self-assessment.

Facilitator assessment. You now take your turn in assessing the same person's competence in the light of the criteria, also with special reference to overplayed, underplayed or omitted strengths and weaknesses in the self-assessment *and* in the peer assessments of that person

Revised self-assessment. The same person takes a further turn to revise their self-assessment, taking into account peer assessments and the facilitator assessment.

Optional: negotiated final self-, peer and facilitator assessment. In this optional extra, you negotiate a final assessment with the person, if your facilitator assessment dissents from their revised self-assessment. The use of this option depends on the subject matter. If it is personal growth that is being assessed, you may judge that self-assessment is primary and the sequence should end with the revised self-assessment. If more external and technical skills are being assessed, there is a case for more facilitator influence and control through your negotiation in the final assessment. You can and should bring in the peers to contribute to this final negotiation.

Each stage requires a precise time allocation, and pacing and time-control need to be well managed. The outcomes for each person can be used to generate action plans for further learning.

If you take a turn along with everyone else in the self- and peer assessments of competence in the selected skill, if you omit the part about commenting on peer assessments, and if you don't claim more weight for your views than for anyone else's, then you have effectively merged collaborative assessment into self- and peer assessment, autonomous mode.

14. Collaborative course evaluation. This combines 11 and 12 and is applied to the whole course. You and the group collaborate in devising a set of procedures - including imaginal methods as in 2, page 67 - for evaluating the whole course, your own role and your use of the six dimensions and three modes, the content of the programme, the use of time, the effectiveness of the methods for learning about the topics, the group process and the learning process, and so on.

15. Co-operative inquiry. You initiate, and invite the group to participate with you in, a co-operative inquiry: a form of person-centred research, in which everyone involved moves between the roles of co-researcher - generating the thinking that conceives, designs, manages and draws conclusions from, the research - and co-subject - engaging in the action and experience which are the focus of the inquiry. People may, of course, undertake many different functions within these two main roles. I and many others have written about this, and I refer the reader to two basic texts (Reason and Rowan, 1981; Reason, 1988).

Any group using the experiential learning cycle systematically, is already engaged in an incipient form of co-operative inquiry: for both methods move cyclically between phases of reflection and phases of action. What co-operative inquiry adds is the focus on systematic inquiry, which takes understanding into issues of valid knowledge. This makes it more rigorous in method, including the use of a whole set of procedures to enhance the validity of the findings as they emerge.

Co-operative inquiry could be used as an advanced stage of experiential learning. Thus when a basic set of skills has been learnt, then the whole conceptual framework which they express - or more likely some feature of it - can be taken into a co-operative inquiry.

In a co-operative inquiry, you start out as the initiating researcher and facilitator; but once the group has internalized the method, you become peer, and all facilitative roles in the inquiry process are rotated among group members.

The meaning dimension: autonomous mode

Here you give no information, no views on issues, no interpretation of events, nor do you elicit from members their own views about some issues you think relevant, or their interpretations about something you have seen. You do nothing that alerts people to the meaning of current issues and events. You leave this entirely to the group members, as and when they feel moved to do so. Making sense is autonomous and self-generated within the group. Often this may be done within a structure given by you: but inside this structure group members are on their own, meaning is self-generated.

1. Self- and peer feedback and reflection. This is the reflection phase in a structured exercise facilitated by you, using the experiential learning cycle, for skills building or any other task in a small group. A key part of the structure is that each person, after taking their turn at practice, gives feedback to self, then receives feedback from peers. If used for skills building, the behaviour is rerun until everyone is satisfied that it is on track. After self- and peer feedback on all the turns, then the small group reflects on the issues that have emerged, distilling further learning from the experience.

This self- and peer feedback and reflection is the central place where meaning is generated autonomously. It is always done in the small practice group, *before* coming back for wider sharing in the large group and with you. Of course, the autonomous feedback may incorporate concepts given by you in introducing the exercise: but when this happens, or whether and how it does, is all in the domain of group autonomy.

2. Self- and peer learning groups. These are small groups for those who are working individually or for those who are doing some task collectively, as a team. In either case, they may be busy with what was agreed in the various learning contracts discussed in 3, 4, 5 and 6, planning dimension, co-operative mode, page 55. For cognitive tasks, people can brainstorm and discuss ideas; share resources, references and information; share work in progress and final drafts for feedback. For skills building, they can use the cycle of practice, feedback, reflection and more practice.

3. Self- and peer imaginal groups. These are small groups for autonomous learning in which members use the full range of imaginal methods - *metaphor, instance, resonance, presentation, dramaturgy, demonstration,* *caricature* - to deepen their understanding of topic, skill or process. These groups may be the same as those in 2 functioning in the imaginal way.

4. Self- and peer supervision groups. These are a little different. Participants meet at intervals in small groups and take it in turns to share some current learning problem, to do with task or process issues or both. Immediately after their turn, each person receives comment, opinion, feedback and suggestions on what has been shared from the other group members, and then makes a final statement taking account of all this, including some action plan for dealing with the problem. Both conceptual and imaginal sorts of understanding can be applied.

5. Self- and peer learning resources. You provide facilities for individual, self-directed learning, and/or peer learning in small groups: libraries, audio-visual aids, CCTV, computer-assisted and computer-managed learning programmes, self-rating questionnaires and inventories, written or taped instructions for structured exercises (task or process oriented) in small groups.

6. Self- and peer intermittent review. After a phase of group life you delegate to group members to do on their own a review of group process, of the learning tasks, and of the learning process - although not necessarily all these three on the same occasion of review.

This autonomous review can be prior to the collaborative reviews described in 11 and 12, co-operative mode, page 72. It can use verbal/conceptual kinds of understanding, or the several imaginal forms described in 2, hierarchical mode, page 67.

7. Self- and peer assessment. In small groups, each member assesses their own competence in skills or other learning, with feedback from peers. This refers back to a whole lot of work done, and is for use at infrequent intervals and at the end of a course. You will need to give group members a structure for doing this, and to train and supervise them in the early use of it, until they become effectively self-directing. The basic stages are:

Autonomous criteria-setting. Group members agree, on their own, on a few basic criteria of competence relevant to the skill being assessed.

Self-assessment. Each individual assesses their own competence, in front of their peers, dealing with strengths and weaknesses in the light of each criterion.

Peer assessment. Group members take it in turn to assess - in the light of each criterion - the competence of the person who has just completed their self-assessment, with special reference to overplayed, underplayed or omitted strengths and weaknesses in the self-assessment.

Revised self-assessment. The same person now takes a further turn to revise their self-assessment, taking into account peer assessments.

Optional: negotiated self- and peer final assessment. In this optional extra, the peers negotiate a final assessment with the person, if they dissent from the revised self-assessment. The use of this option depends on the subject matter. If it is personal growth that is being assessed, it seems that self-assessment is primary and the sequence should end with the revised self-assessment. If more external and technical skills are being assessed, there is a case for more peer influence and control through their negotiation in the final assessment.

Each stage requires a precise time allocation, and pacing and time control need to be well managed. This is a rigorous and demanding procedure which visibly matures those who apply themselves to it.

It can be used entirely on its own, as described, with you the facilitator absent, or with you sitting in but not participating at all (except in early stages for supervision of the procedure). Or it can be used within collaborative assessment as in 13, co-operative mode, page 72. In either case, each person can use its outcomes to generate an action plan for further learning.

8. Self- and peer learning-analysis. This is a weak form of self- and peer assessment. Each member in turn takes the focal role and listens to everyone else say what that person would be doing if he were learning with optimal effectiveness. He then responds with his own self-assessment, reacting to the comments of each of his peers.

9. Peer review audit. This is self- and peer assessment applied to professional work in the world: it can be used on day release, in-service professional development training groups. The purpose of peer review audit is for professionals in an entirely self-directed way to generate and maintain standards of excellence in performance on the job.

It will usually be done by a small group of those doing the same kind of work. The group will need some training and supervision by you to acquire the competence to do this exercise effectively. The stages are as follows:

Analyse job. The group members break down the work into its component parts, and choose one part of it to audit.

Agree criteria. They decide on a small number of basic criteria of what it is to do that part of the work well.

Devise self- (and peer) assessment. They work out a way of sampling their daily work of this kind, of assessing it in the light of the agreed criteria, and of keeping some record of these self-assessments. Where people work together, the self-assessment can be extended to include some form of peer assessment on the job. These first three stages can all be done in one meeting of the group, on the day release course.

On the job self- (and peer) assessment. They get on with their professional work for an agreed period of days or weeks using the self-assessments, with peer assessments where possible, on work samples, and keeping records of all these.

Feedback on assessment. The group have a second meeting on the day release course and each one takes it in turns to share the self- and peer assessments on his performance with the rest of the group. Each presenter gets feedback from the other group members, being confronted on avoided weaknesses, and supported on underplayed or omitted strengths: interpersonal skill is needed here. The presenter then reviews his overall self-assessment in the light of this feedback; this may lead over into a personal action-plan to take account of the findings.

Planning the next cycle. The group members now decide whether to start a second cycle continuing to assess performance on the same part of the job. If so, they review the criteria, methods of sampling, assessment and record-keeping, the amount of time spent on the job between feedback meetings; they may change some of these. If not, then they choose some other part of the job and go through the whole procedure on that.

On the job self- (and peer) assessment etc. This process can continue indefinitely. In practice, a group will prefer to use it for a certain number of cycles, then apply the learning for quite a long period without further audit (Heron, 1981).

9. Autonomous co-operative inquiry. As in 15, co-operative mode, page 73, except that it excludes you, the facilitator. This would be at an advanced stage in a group's history, after it had learned to do co-operative inquiry with you.

10. No interpretation phase. You stop giving interpretations or prompting the group to interpret. You wait to see if group members will generate their own meanings. This sort of lying low can be covert and unannounced, or you can say that you are doing it and for how long it will continue.

11. Autonomous monitoring of meaning. In this extension of the initiative clause (see 9, planning dimension, autonomous mode, page 60) into the meaning dimension, you have created a climate of shared leadership, in which group members spontaneously give meaning to what is happening, alongside your management of this dimension.

12. Trainer-trainee delegation. You appoint one person in the group, or in each of several sub-groups, to exercise the interpretative role, with feedback on the interpretations afterwards from the other members. This, of course, is an exercise in a training the trainers' group.

13. Self-generated insight. Some systems of growth and therapy (e.g. primal therapy, co-counselling) believe that the only really authentic interpretations of a psychodynamic kind are those that arise spontaneously within the individual in the course of their personal growth work. This work may be actively facilitated, but you, the facilitator, never make any interpretations, and make sure space is given for the client to verbalise self-generated insights as they arise. So while your facilitation, especially with respect to release of feeling, is hierarchical and co-operative, so far as meaning is concerned only client insights count.

14. Autonomous personal meaning groups. A whole group may be run in such a way that the personal meaning dimension is entirely autonomous, dealt with by self- and peer feedback on skills practice and/or self-generated insight in personal growth work. By personal meaning, I refer to the meaning that is given to individual experience and behaviour. Such a group, however, may well have some general theory inputs (hierarchical mode), which provide concepts which members may later use when generating their own personal meanings.

5. The confronting dimension

The confronting aspect of facilitation is to do with how to raise consciousness about resistances to, and avoidances of, things that need to be faced and dealt with. Because of such resistance and avoidance, there is a block, a rigidity, a restriction in the dynamic of the group, so that learning is distorted or held back.

What is being resisted and avoided will be something to do with one or more of the threatening issues referred to in Chapter 2: authority and control, conflict and aggression, intimacy and contact, love and care, sexuality and gender, identity and purpose, disclosure and expression, truth and honesty, mastery and competence or knowledge and ignorance.

Sources of rigidity

What the nature of the resisting and avoiding is, takes us back to Chapter 2. There I looked at three negative forms of the group dynamic, each giving a different perspective on resistant rigidity in the group. I will mention them again briefly here, and add two further sources of such blockage.

1. Educational alienation. If the group is limited to just one kind of learning objective, then its members can become rigid and alienated in their way of being: intellect cut off from feelings and the spirit; feelings cut off from the intellect and the spirit; the spirit cut off from both intellect and feelings; etc.

2. Cultural oppression. Group behaviour is constrained into resistant blocks by oppressive norms and values which members bring with them from the surrounding culture.

3. Psychological defensiveness. Group behaviour is seized into distorted, defensive forms by an uprush of existential and archaic anxieties - arising from unowned present and past distress - which are stirred up by being in the group.

4. Underdevelopment. Group members lack knowledge, competence and cultivated awareness - in the area of some special skills, or about group process, or about the learning process, or all of these. Such ignorance creates its own kind of blind, resistant inertia.

5. Easy street. Group members go for the soft option, the familiar ground, the comfortable and the convenient. This is basically an avoidance of risk taking, the preference for no challenge: the lotus-eating, pleasure-seeking rigidity.

Of course, these five processes overlap and reinforce each other. But there are times when each one of them can appear quite noticeably in its own right, even though one or more of the others will be somewhere in the background.

Elements and purposes of confrontation

When you, the facilitator, want to confront any of these five processes, there are three things about which you can raise group members' consciousness, and three purposes you may have in mind in so doing:

The issue. You want the group members to become aware of the issue being avoided, so that they can address it and move the learning into it.

The rigid behaviour. You also want them to become aware of the sort of behaviour that is doing the avoiding, so that they can see it for what it is and abandon it for more adventurous forms.

The source. Then you want them to identify the source of that behaviour - in limited learning objectives, or cultural norms, or past distress, of lack of knowledge, or pursuit of ease - so that they have more command over it.

You can focus on one or other of these three, or on all of them: they are interdependent. Sometimes it is enough to mention the first one: raising awareness about the issue that is being avoided breaks the block, resistance ceases and members take up the challenge. It may not be necessary to deal with the other two things.

At other times members may have clearly to identify the rigidity and become aware of its source, before they can dislodge themselves from it. In the more extreme case, some resistant behaviour may be so rooted in, for example, archaic distress, that you have to take time out to do personal growth work on this source before you can get any behavioural shift toward the issue. However, confrontation *per se* is concerned with effecting a behavioural shift by consciousness-raising alone.

The process of confrontation

You need to be respectful and affirmative of persons while being uncompromising about the issue and the rigid behaviour. The ideal is to tell the truth with love, without being the least judgmental, moralistic, oppressive or nagging. You are not attached to what you say: you can let it go as well as hold firmly and uncompromisingly to it.

Because you know the confrontation may be received by group members as something of a shock, the thought of delivering it may make you anxious. If this perfectly normal present-time anxiety gets compounded by archaic anxiety - from old, unfinished confronting agendas of your past - then all this may distort your confronting behaviour in one of two directions, as shown in figure 5.1.

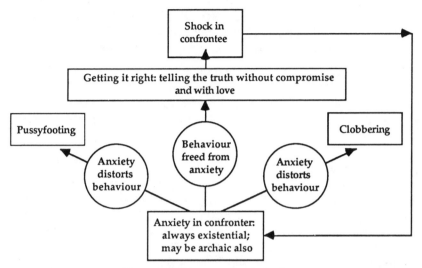

Figure 5.1 *The process of confrontation*

At one extreme, you may soft-pedal the delivery, skirt round the issue, and shirk unmasking fully the rigid behaviour; or at worst, you may simply not make the confrontation at all. At the other extreme, you may become heavy-handed, bludgeoning the group in a punitive way.

The first is avoidance behaviour, the second attack behaviour - both are distortions coming out of your compound anxiety, from which you have not managed to free your intervention.

The challenge is to get it right: too much love and you collude; too much power and you oppress. You are on the razor's edge between the two.

Confronting and meaning

In several of the interventions below, the confronting and meaning dimensions directly overlap: the strategy - an interpretation - is of the same sort as one in the meaning dimension, but it is also used to shock and awaken people out of their unaware, rigid state.

Nevertheless, the two dimensions are distinct: many other interventions on the meaning dimension have no, and are not intended to have any, confronting impact. Making sense of experience is much wider that uncovering defensive states of mind and behaviour.

Cycles of expansion and contraction

While the group is moving from the stage of defensiveness to the stage of authentic behaviour, as described in Chapter 2, it will go through typical cycles of expansion and contraction. When the initial rigidity is successfully confronted and the underlying issue faced, then the group process expands in a phase of open learning. After a while, another kind of rigidity comes to the fore, the group process contracts, and the cycle is repeated.

So the need for confronting interventions is periodic. There are phases when the climate needs to be safe and supportive to maximize learning, and at these times it is inappropriate to confront. If you do so, you are getting lost in some counter-transference, or misjudging the state of the group dynamic.

One-to-group and one-to-one

This dimension corresponds, for the group, to one-to-one *confronting* in my *Six Category Intervention Analysis* (Heron, 1989). You will find there a four-part analysis of one-to-one confronting, and a list of interventions. Please note in that book I call unaware, distorted and defensive behaviours and attitudes, and the issues to which they relate, 'agendas'. Also note that in the one-to-one context with which that book deals, threatening issues will not arise in the same sort of way that they do in a group. For the individual client in a one-to-one setting, many agendas will arise because they are an issue for that person in their current everyday life. However, transference, which I discuss in Chapter 2 of this book, is a process that occurs in both one-to-group and one-to-one settings.

The two contexts also become similar if a group goes in for much personal growth work *per se*, independent of group-related issues. A very wide range of individual agendas indeed may then come forward. The facilitator and the person working are effectively in a one-to-one setting and the six category analysis of confronting applies.

The interventions below are for the context of groups and group-related issues.

The confronting dimension: hierarchical mode

Here you directly interrupt the rigid behaviour, and point to the issue which that behaviour is busy avoiding. You do this in such a way that those concerned may take up the issue, and thereby show some awareness of their avoidance.

You are doing this to people and for people, entirely in the hierarchical mode. Any particular unilateral confrontation is by definition unsolicited: it points to something the group is unware of, and so cannot ask to be helped with. But it is legitimated by the implicit warrant of your role: it is the sort of thing a facilitator is expected to do. This warrant, for any given group and its objectives, does have limits, however, and you need to be clear in your own mind what these limits are.

Give time, after a confrontation, for people to assimilate the shock of it and to explore their reactions to it. Interrupt any return to compulsive avoidance and denial. Help people own their defensive process and see it for what it is.

If only one or two group members are involved, you may wish to move over into the co-operative mode, gather in feedback from other people in the group and have a general sharing of views.

1. Confronting interpretation. You *interrupt* the resistant behaviour - of one or some or all of the group - and identify it as a way of not dealing with some issue. This is done in a manner that is supportive of the persons concerned, uncompromising about the behaviour.

Issue focus. You may say: 'I think we are all avoiding issue X.' So you go straight for the avoided issue, without focussing on how it is being avoided. The immediate challenge of the issue may loosen people from their resistant block.

Avoidance focus. You may say: 'I think this behaviour Q is a way of avoiding something.' You spotlight the process of resistance. You may do this for its own sake, to facilitate learning about human behaviour, or you may not be clear what the issue is, although the avoidance of something is obvious. Alternatively, you may sense what the issue is, but judge that it is too heavy to go for it straight away: so you start with the avoidance first, then move on to the issue.

Source focus. You may say: 'I think cultural norm F is invading the group, getting us stuck in behaviour Q as a way of avoiding something.' You identify the avoidance behaviour, but the main focus is on where it comes from. You judge it is important to raise consciousness about the source of the resistance, then go on to the issue that is being avoided.

All of it. You may say: 'I think cultural norm F is invading the group, getting us stuck in behaviour Q as a way of avoiding issue X.' This is the full-blown confronting interpretation. This may be the one that raises consciousness to the point of addressing issue X. But if it seems it would be too much to cope with, then proceed gradually, as above.

The kinds of interpretation used in the above are mostly psychodynamic and sociodynamic, with elements of the attributive. See the meaning dimension, hierarchical mode, page 68.

They can also be supplemented, or even entirely replaced, by interpretations given in one or other of the imaginal forms - *metaphor, instance, resonance, presentation, dramaturgy, demonstration* and *caricature* - as these are defined in 2, meaning dimension, hierarchical mode, page 67.

2. Objective confrontation. The interpretations in 1 can be delivered in an 'objective' form, as a straight declaration of what is going on in the group. But it is still supportive: non-punitive and non-moralistic. It is given as information to be used; not as condemnation and heavy-handed judgment.

3. Subjective confrontation. The interpretations can also be given in a more diffident, 'subjective' mode: 'For what it is worth, right or wrong, my impression is that ...'. This version may express a real uncertainty about the content of the interpretation, or it may be used to gain a hearing about a very sensitive issue. Again, it is supportive and non-punitive.

4. Confronting theory. You present some *general* ideas which raise consciousness about *personal* or *group* defensiveness. For example, aspects of the group dynamic theory raised in Chapter 2. You may then apply the ideas to current or recent defensive events in the group.

5. Confronting action. When confronting one or more persons, or the group as a whole, you propose an action - doing or saying something - that challenges and interrupts the defensive behaviour in those concerned. There are two versions:

> *Issue focus.* The action brings the person directly to grips with the issue they have been avoiding. So you may ask someone to declare attraction directly to those for whom it is felt.

> *Source focus.* The action takes the person into the source of the avoidance. You could, therefore, ask the same person to declare their fear of owning and dealing with such attraction - and make associations between this fear and events in their past history.

6. Contractual confrontation. This confrontation invokes a contract made with the group - about objectives, methods, ground-rules of interaction or of group discipline - to interrupt behaviour that is both breaking the contract and avoiding some issue. You challenge the offenders to abide by the contract and address the issue, or to give good reason for renegotiating the contract. In the extreme case, you can add the third alternative, which is to leave the group.

7. Skills feedback confrontation. In a skills training group, a trainee may have great difficulty in acquiring a new piece of behaviour, through some combination of habit, inertia, lack of awareness, social embarrassment and perhaps deeper levels of defensiveness. With a light and loving touch, you keep homing in with feedback on the bits of behaviour that go wrong, keep modelling how to do them, and keep the trainee rerunning the practice until it starts to come right. This purely behavioural feedback and remodelling can be effective without going into the dynamics of defensiveness.

8. Disagreeing and correcting. This is the traditional cognitive kind of confrontation, in which you disagree with what is being said and correct it. You interrupt, and raise consciousness about, errors and confusions of understanding. This needs to be followed by a co-operative discussion that leads either to final agreement or respectful disagreement.

9. Discharge confrontation. Free from any explicitly stated attack, invalidation or negative feedback, you discharge fully in sound (no words) and movement your pent-up anger and frustration generated by blocking and avoidance behaviour in the group. A radical but effective strategy if the situation merits it and provided you can enter into a constructive, caring interaction with those concerned immediately afterwards.

The confronting dimension: co-operative mode

You work *with* the group and its members to raise consciousness about avoided issues, resistant behaviour and its sources - by prompting people to do this to some degree for themselves. You invite and ask them, consult them and compare and share views with them.

When only one or some of the group are involved, you ask them first, then gather in views from the non-involved, and finally add your own. This is followed by general discussion. An important and special case is when it is your own behaviour that needs confronting.

1. Inviting a confronting interpretation. Where some or all of the group are resistant and blocked, you invite those concerned to come forward with their own account of the threatening issue, or of the avoidance behaviour, or of the source of this behaviour, or of some combination of these. You then ask for the views of the others. You may then add your own view as one among many. This is collective and co-operative consciousness-raising. The verbal form of this intervention, when addressed to those concerned, is: 'I would like to suggest that you consider whether you are avoiding any issue now; and if so, what it is, how you may be avoiding it, and what the sources of that avoidance may be.' You may deal with these four points - whether, what, how, why - gradually rather than all at once.

2. Confronting questioning. This is a more head-on technique. You can put a straight, direct question that interrupts the resistant behaviour, and asks those concerned to raise their own consciousness about it. Aiming the question is in the hierarchical mode, but the main *intent* of the question is co-operative: to prompt, encourage, and elicit; to invite the recipient to participate in uncovering the learning.

Issue focus. Your question asks the group or person to identify the issue that is being avoided: 'What are you busy *not* dealing with/owning/saying?' The thrust of this question can be framed in many different ways.

Avoidance focus. Your question asks whether the behaviour you have interrupted has some evasive function: 'Is what you are doing or saying a way of avoiding dealing with something else?'

Source focus. Here your question asks about the origins of the resistant behaviour: 'Where do you imagine this avoidance behaviour comes from?'

All of it. Your question puts it all together: 'Is what you are doing or saying a way of avoiding somethind; if so, what are you not dealing with; and what is the source of the avoidance?'

3. Contractual query. You put a question to those whose unaware behaviour is breaking a contract made with the group - about objectives, methods, ground-rules of interaction or of group discipline - and thereby also avoiding some issue: 'What are you avoiding by breaking the group's agreement to....?'

4. Competence query. In skills training practice your question for the client who can't get it right is: 'Can you identify exactly what it is you do that keeps you off track?' Or: 'What precisely do you need to do to get it right?' After you get an answer, you can ask other members of the practice group to give their feedback and comment.

5. Cognitive query. For someone in a state of mental error, confusion or contradiction, you ask: 'Is that really how you understand it?' Or: 'What is it you are busy trying not to understand?'

6. Putting them to the group. Where one or two or more members are locked unawares in some avoidance behaviour, you invite others in the group to confront what is going on. Several overlapping confrontations may be given, to which you may or may not add your own. This, too, is co-operative and collective consciousness-raising, in which the recipients are invited to participate.

7. Descriptive confrontation. You simply make a descriptive comment about the avoidance behaviour, without attaching any kind of interpretation to it, or without asking anyone to interpret it. 'You have spent 20 minutes criticizing this room.' This may, or may not, lead to some airing of views by group members about whether the described behaviour is avoiding something, and if so, what, and maybe even why.

8. Indicative confrontation. This is the same as 7, except that you don't pick out the avoidance behaviour verbally, but non-verbally, by gesture, touch, the direction of the gaze. This invites imaginal understanding first of all.

9. Invite mythic confrontation. Ask group members to use metaphor, allegory, phantasy, fable or story, to give an account of the avoided issue, the avoidance behaviour and its possible source, and so generate imaginal understanding of these. You join in the sharing and discussion of myths.

10. Invite confrontation by resonance. Invite group members to share any associations and memories evoked by avoidance behaviour in the group, in order to find meaning through resonance with the form of other situations. You share you own associations, and join in the general discussion.

11. Invite presentational confrontation. You invite one or more members to give imaginal meaning to the avoided issue, the avoidance behaviour and its possible source, by symbolizing these non-verbally in movement, a group sculpture made of body postures, vocal sounds or instrumental music, a painting or drawing. You add your own portrayal. Feedback on these presentations may then lead on to a verbal sharing that includes you; so the group moves from imaginal to conceptual understanding. This may relate to either task or process.

12. Invite dramaturgical confrontation. You suggest that the confrontation is portrayed through mime, or a piece of theatre with dramatic dialogue. You participate in the creation of this, its execution and the following discussion.

13. Invite mimicry confrontation. You invite group members to mimic and caricature a piece of avoidance behaviour, with supportive attention, and without mockery or malice, so that those concerned become more aware about it by seeing it as if in a mirror. You may then do the same. This may be followed by some of the other interventions above.

13. Distract and interrupt. You distract people from, and also cut right across, their unaware avoidance behaviour, and so indirectly raise in them a question mark as to what it is all about. You may do this in many different ways: by a change of topic or activity, by totally shifting group attention to someone else, by moving very close to those involved, by touching them in a friendly way, etc.

14. Conflict resolution. A special case of avoidance behaviour is when two group members become locked in unproductive conflict. If raising their consciousness about the avoided issue does not get them out of it, then you may invite them to participate in a conflict resolution exercise which you facilitate. The first thing is to free them from their emotional fixation so that they can understand each other's point of view and deal with the issues, rather than hysterically defend their ground. There are three classic techniques. They are given in order of depth of intervention.

Controlled discussion. You umpire an exchange of views with two rules: each person makes only one point at a time; and each restates the other's point to the other's satisfaction before making a point in reply. This takes the heat out of the discussion, and starts listening and relating.

Role reversal. You umpire an exchange of views. When the tension rises, have the pair reverse roles so that they represent fully their opponent's point of view. Then switch them back to themselves. Repeat until the debate moves towards rationality and resolution.

Hidden agenda counselling. Ask each person what it is they really need from the other. Do this by asking them to address an empty chair as if it were the other person and complete several times the question 'What I really want from you is ...'. This may uncover some hidden agenda - projected personal and private unfinished business with someone from the past - that is nothing to do with the real issues and the actual situation.

The second thing is to adjudicate co-operative problem-solving. Take the pair through a problem-solving cycle.

Diagnosis. Prompt them to state the problem clearly and agree the degree to which each of them is responsible, and what the other causes, if any, are.

Treatment. Help them to identify possible solutions, assess each one in terms of its probable outcomes, choose one of them, and make an appropriate action plan to implement it.

Follow-up. Invite them to contract to meet at a future date and review the action taken, its effectiveness in dealing with the problem, and the current status of the problem.

The confronting dimension: autonomous mode

Here you do not work in the confronting mode either directly, or indirectly by prompting, but create a climate of safety, support and trust, so that the challenge to dismantle defences occurs independently within the group or the individual. It may be that structures given by you enable group members to practise self- and peer confrontation. So we have:

1. Structured peer confrontation. You set up a structured exercise in which participants confront each other in small groups. The confrontation may relate to issues that have been avoided, how and from what source - in the large group, or to issues currently being avoided in the small groups. Or the exercise may be for the purpose of building up confronting skills by role playing imaginary scenarios.

2. Structured self-confrontation. You set up an exercise in which each person takes it in turns, in small groups, to confront themselves about what issues they are currently avoiding, how they are avoiding them, and what the source of the avoidance seems to be. Again this can relate back to the large group, or currently to the small group. This exercise can be done 'pure', with no peer feedback, or it can be combined with 1, in which case it works best if the self-confrontation precedes the peer confrontation.

3. Devil's advocate. You establish a ground rule whereby it is open to anyone at any time to announce they are going to assume the role of devil's advocate. They put on a special hat, or hold a 'mace', to indicate they are in the devil's advocate role. They may then expose hidden issues, avoidance behaviour and possible sources of it. This piece of theatre enables the devil's advocate to raise a confrontation issue more in a spirit of inquiry and creative challenge. All kinds of doubts, uncertainties and uneasinesses about the group dynamic can be dealt with in this way, without the advocate fully identifying with them or officially holding them. The theatre also places the listeners at some distance from what is being said so that they can consider it more carefully.

4. No confrontation phase. You stop confronting or prompting the group to confront. You wait to see if group members will generate their own confronting. This phase can be covert and unnanounced, or you can say that you are doing it and for how long it will take place..

5. Autonomous monitoring of avoidance. In this extension of the initiative clause (see 9, planning dimension, autonomous mode, page 60) into the confronting dimension, you have created a climate of shared leadership, in which group members spontaneously confront avoided issues and resistant behaviour, alongside your management of this dimension.

6. Trainer-trainee delegation. You appoint one person in the group, or in each of several sub-groups, to exercise the confronting role, with feedback on the interpretations afterwards from the other members. This, of course, is an exercise in a training the trainers' group.

7. Tense silence. An unannounced and impromptu autonomy phase, in which you respond to mounting tension within the group with silence, waiting for the group to implode into confronting its own process.

8. Backing off. When one or more persons, or the group as a whole, is highly defensive and is resisting dealing with your confrontation, you suddenly drop it entirely, and switch over to some quite different matter. The effect is to increase the internal pressure toward self-confrontation - about the abandoned issue - in those concerned.

9. Confrontation resources. CCTV with playback is a resource which the group can use on its own to confront its own process. Individuals too can use it on their own to confront their own more personal defensive behaviour, evident in frame-by-frame exposure of micro-cues. Self-rating instruments, and questionnaires for the group, can also be used.

10. Self- and peer confrontation group. The group is run in such a way that all the confrontation is done by self or peer and never by you. You make it explicit that you will function on the other dimensions but not on the confronting dimension. This model presupposes that you have already included in the group programme some demonstration of and training in confronting strategies.

11. Self-confrontation only. You create a climate of safety and support in the group, with a ground rule that there is no person-to-person, and no person-to-group, confrontation, but only internal, self-confrontation. This presupposes that group members have had some kind of training in purely self-directed personal development work, and each one is very sharp at interrupting their own projections on to others. Once a group is capable of functioning in this way, it doesn't really need you. The so-called independent group in co-counselling would be a limited example: each person taking a turn to be a self-directed client - interrupting their own defensive processes - with supportive attention, but no interventions, from the group. It is limited because the structure prohibits any interpersonal work from going on.

Psychological somnambulism is a chronic habit in human behaviour: the tendency to fall asleep in interactions with others without awareness of one's behaviour, its effects and its motives. Hence we need, with much supportive rigour, to help each other wake up from time to time.

6. The feeling dimension

This dimension is concerned with the management of feeling. For you, the facilitator, the question is how to handle the emotional life of the group - the heart of its dynamic.

Positive emotional processes

There are at least seven basic constructive emotional processes, each requiring *awareness*. One or more of them will be at the heart of the group dynamic when authentic behaviour of one sort or another - as outlined in Chapter 2 - is going on. Each of them is healthy, valid and appropriate in its proper context.

1. Identification. A person knows what emotional state they are in and can identify the feelings involved, can experience them, and owns them.

2. Acceptance. A person both identifies/experiences/owns their feelings *and* accepts them.

3. Control. A person awarely controls their emotional state, without either denying it or suppressing it, in order to accomplish some task, or interact appropriately with other persons.

4. Redirection. A person awarely directs an aroused feeling into a channel other than its normal outlet. Thus a person who is angry about an interruption of their activity, may for good reason choose to direct the energy of the anger into some vigorous competitive sport.

5. Switching. A person awarely chooses to change an emotional state by switching attention off it and its context, on to some other activity and outlook which generate a different emotional state. As a result of switching, one sort of feeling gives way to a different one. You can switch *laterally*, from an emotional state on the ordinary level of consciousness to another state on the same level; or you can switch *vertically*, from a state on the ordinary level to a state on a higher level of consciousness.

6. Transmutation. A person awarely chooses to sublimate and refine an emotional state so that it is internally transformed. This is the psychological alchemy of turning base metal into gold. A classic method is to hold the light of awareness intently and constantly within a negative emotional state, until its dross is transfigured.

Let me underline the difference between redirection, switching and transmutation.

Redirection. The feeling continues to be present, but its energy is given some alternative outlet to the one it would normally seek. So anger is redirected into competitive sport rather than let out in protest at being interrupted.

Switching. The feeling falls into the background because some other feeling is intentionally generated in the foreground. So the anger recedes because choosing to attend some quite different situation and outlook brings exhilaration to the fore.

Transmutation. The feeling internally changes its nature and becomes a different feeling: the frequency of its energy is entirely altered. So anger, by the transformative, focussed action of consciousness, *becomes* peace.

7. Catharsis. A person awarely chooses to discharge distress emotions - grief, fear, anger - through, respectively, tears, trembling, high frequency sound and movement. The painful feeling is released from the mind and body; and this generates spontaneous insight into origins and subsequent effects.

8. Expression. A person awarely gives verbal and physical expression to their feelings, to celebrate, affirm and bear witness to the joy and drama of their unique existence.

Experiential learning, in its affective dimension, is concerned to help people acquire skills in the exercise of all these processes, shown in figure 6.1.

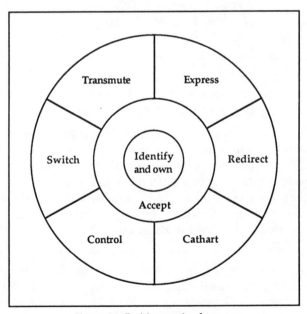

Figure 6.1 *Positive emotional processes*

Negative emotional processes

There are eight, roughly corresponding, negative emotional processes:

1. Alienation. A person is cut off from their emotional state and cannot identify what it is. Asked about their feelings, they will talk about their thoughts.

2. Suppression. A person identifies their emotional state only enough to subject themselves to instantaneous social inhibition.

3. Fixation. A person is stuck in some emotional state, either fascinated by it in a morbid way or sunk in it with depressive inertia. Their awareness is a slave of the state and cannot (or, more properly, feels unwilling to make the effort to) move out of it.

4. Displacement. A distress emotion is displaced unawarely into some action that is maladaptive, socially inappropriate and disturbing, or into some negative attitude toward the self. The distress emotion involved is usually also repressed.

5. Distraction. Emotional states fluctuate in a disoriented way because the person is being chaotically distracted by one stimulus after another, coming from some mixture of the mind and the external world.

6. Degradation. An emotional state is debased into a lesser or lower or more negative one, by indulging in it in a distorted way.

7. Dramatization. A distress emotion is displaced into pseudo-catharsis. The outlet has elements of the hysterical or the rigid. The distress slips out of the true cathartic channel, and distorts itself on the way out.

8. Repression. Distress emotions are pushed out of consciousness and their presence in the mind is denied. Then we have the return of the repressed in distorted form. Most of the so-called defence mechanisms are a combination of repression and 4, displacement.

Experiential learning, in its affective dimension, is concerned to help people acquire skills in identifying all these negative processes, in interrupting them, and in transforming their energy and integrating it with positive processes.

The role of pathology

There are psychotherapies that aim to clean you up: their goal is to get rid of the pathology, the distress, the misbegotten behaviour, and restore you to fully integrated, healthy human functioning. There have been Reich's genital character, Janov's post-primal man, the rational distress-free human of re-evaluation counselling - and so on.

There are others, however, which see the dark side of human nature as a complement to the light, and seek to accept and include it, reclaiming its energies from rejection, denial and hostility. Thus the concept of integrating the shadow in Jungian psychology (Jung, 1964). And Hillman, in his archetypal psychology, sees the tendency of the soul continuously to pathologize its existence in different areas, as the leading edge of its growth: it generates new patches of disturbance in order to deepen its maturity (Hillman, 1975).

The distinction is roughly that between perfectionism and holism - which could also be called organicism. The former seeks to get rid of the chaos and create a being without disorder. The latter seeks to integrate and transform the dross, acknowledging it as a *continuous* source of growth, creating a developing whole being, not a perfect one.

Holism sees intermittent chaos as the fertile soil of new levels of organisation and order. My own view of these two ideologies is the paradoxical one that perfectionism is itself a pathology - a defence against holism.

Feeling and the group dynamic

The group dynamic, discussed in detail in Chapter 2, could also be called the emotional dynamic: it is grounded in the life of feeling - which is at the core of the group's state of being. The positive emotional processes, listed above, will be present in differing combinations at the heart of the group dynamic when it is in one of its seven basic positive forms, described on pages 27-28: task-oriented, process-oriented, expressive, interactive, confronting, personal work oriented, charismatic.

And the negative emotional processes listed above will be present in differing combinations when the group dynamic is in one of the five negative forms I have so far considered: educationally alienated, culturally restricted, psychologically defensive, underdeveloped, and in easy streeet. These were last briefly defined on page 79.

The group dynamic is always a mixture of positive and negative emotional processes, positive and negative forms. This is its necessary destiny. To refer back to the stages of the group dynamic described in Chapter 2, pages 26-27, the third, summertime stage of authentic behaviour is never free of negative emotional processes.

On the contrary, these provide an important part of the humus for nourishing its growth. It is just that, compared to earlier stages, the balance of negative and positive is different. In the early stages, the negative processes and forms tended to block the positive; in the third stage, the negative are used like fuel to kindle growth and empower the positive.

The feeling dimension: hierarchical mode

You take charge of the emotional dynamic of the group, directing its process and deciding how the feeling life of the group will be handled. You think *for* the group, judging what ways of managing feelings will suit its members and its purpose best. This means that you identify what the current emotional dynamic is, and decide whether to stay with it and extend or deepen it, or change it.

1. Instruction: identify, own and accept. In the very early stages of a group, especially with beginners in emotional education, you will need, when people show signs of alienation and suppression of feeling, to instruct and advise them to identify, own and accept their emotional states.

2. Attributing feeling. As an alternative, you attribute to one or more group members a feeling state which is unnoticed by them. This is the same as attributive interpretation, given under the meaning dimension, page 64. It may also be a confronting attribution; or it may not, since not every case of someone not noticing their feelings is defensive - it may be just be a conventional lack of awareness.

3. Instruction: aware control. As feelings come up in a group and need to be processed, not everyone can do this work at the same time. You will need to instruct people to learn the art of conscious control: to identify and own the feelings, not to suppress or repress or displace them, but to put them awarely on hold, while they wait their turn, or play some other part in the proceedings.

4. Switch. You take charge of this process, and do it for the group. This is one of the most basic of all interventions for altering the group dynamic. Your intention is to change the being, the feeling state of the group, or of one or more persons in it, by proposing some verbal or non-verbal behaviour that switches attention away from the current state and generates another one. You may suggest a task or change of task, a structured skills building exercise, a theory session, some process analysis, a verbal round, a set of movements, body work, hyperventilation, an active game, a song, a dance, a shout, a break, a ritual, a meditation, and so on.

Switching may be used to take the group from negative to positive states. Within positive states, it may be used to shift the dynamic, either way, between passive and active states, cathartic and outgoing states, low and high energy states, transcendental and grounded states, task and process states, intellectual and experiential states, task states of different kinds and so on. Special cases of switching are opening and closing a group, starting and ending a day or a session.

Switching aids confluent, holistic learning and prevents alienation. Holistic learning means creating equipoise between different kinds of learning. This requires multiplicity, variety and complementarity or contrast - the play of opposities - all in good measure. So there is a balance of several, varied and contrasted activities - within one strand and as between diverse strands of the curriculum. You use switching to orchestrate this balance.

Note that while switching includes other interventions listed in this and other dimensions, not every use of these same interventions is for purposes of switching: they may be used to sustain or develop a state of being, not change it.

5. Giving permission for catharsis. At an early stage in the group's history, you announce with benign authority that catharsis is acceptable, human and healing. You clearly give permission for catharsis to occur, encourage members to accept it when it arises, and give a rationale of its benefits. This permission-giving is directed at the hurt child within - who really needs to hear support and encouragement for the discharge of its pain. This is a basic hierarchical strategy.

6. Lowering the cathartic threshold. Here you take the whole group toward catharsis, by proposing an activity which releases emotional distress in some group members, and lowers the threshold of release in all. The activity may be to do with breathing and body work, with the use of psychodrama, with deep reverie and active imagination. You explain beforehand what the exercise is intended to achieve, and reinforce your permission-giving statements.

7. Charismatic leadership. You take the group into various altered states of consciousness through ritual, mudras, mantras, charismatic song and dance. This opens up the group dynamic to the influences of a vast sphere of subtle energies and enhanced awareness.

8. Transmutation. You propose work on emotional states by transmutative methods in which you are directive, for example in a guided phantasy using archetypal symbols. For further details of transmutation and transmutative interventions see *Six Category Intervention Analysis* (Heron, 1989).

9. Expression and celebration. You propose and direct an activity, for one or more members, or for all the group, as a means of expressing, symbolising, celebrating their state of being. It may be song and music making, dance and movement, drawing and painting, story telling, dramaturgy: imaginal methods (page 67) will be to the fore. There will be affirmations, validations and appreciations.

The expression may celebrate one's own state of being, someone else's, relationships, art, nature, work, humanity, the planet or other realities. It may involve interpersonal declarations and explorations.

This expression of feeling may not only be celebratory but also in the minor key: elegiac, dramatic. It may be defiant, bold, and so on. It may be in the charismatic and spiritual domain.

The feeling dimension: co-operative mode

You work with the group, eliciting, prompting, encouraging and indicating different ways of managing feelings. You are not managing the emotional dynamic of the group for the group, but facilitating co-operative management - you with them.

1. Acting into owning. One or more group members are invited by *you* to say or do something which enables *them* to identify and own unnoticed feelings.

2. Consensus about the emotional dynamic. You prompt the group, by some questions, to identify its emotional state. Is the dynamic positive, outgoing and task-oriented, or inward, brooding and process-oriented, or locked in negative emotional states, or near the release of authentic distress, or subtly attuned to altered states, or something else? You share your views and co-operate in an emerging consensus.

3. Negotiating the emotional process. You invite the group to choose the positive emotional process which it needs to use, either to sustain its current dynamic or to change it. You discuss with the group whether it is time to identify, control, redirect, switch, transmute, cathart or express feelings. You share your view as one among many. You may need to prompt the group, remind them of possibilities. But the outcome is a shared choice.

4. Negotiating the emotional method. After agreeing on the process, you then negotiate with the group on the method it will adopt to switch, cathart, express or whatever you have chosen to do. Again, you may need to prompt the group with a reminder of the range of options, before you and they choose one together. This intervention is also a co-operative one on the structuring dimension.

The decision-procedure, in 2, 3 and 4 here, will usually be one in which you 'gather the sense of the meeting' after a sufficient number, including yourself, have spoken. These three strategies need a light touch, keeping the business elegant, not ponderous and protracted.

5. Individual work. You invite one person to do some cathartic work, releasing emotional pain, in the middle of the group, supported by group energy and attention and facilitated by you. This always involves *co-operation* between you and the individual concerned, since it is based on their freely given assent and choice, and proceeds by a subtle midwifery from you that interacts with cues the person is already emitting.

This person may already be on the brink - tearful, or trembling, or tense with anger - triggered by something going on in the group. Or they may simply report (whether casually or more substantially) on some problem or difficulty, while still cut off from the underlying distress. If the person gives a double message, of both wanting and not wanting to do the work, keep putting out the invitation until an unequivocal 'yes' or 'no' is forthcoming. If the final response is 'no', then respect this: no-one should ever be pressured into catharsis. Each person must choose and has a right to choose the moment for lowering their defences.

The work, of course, may involve other growth processes as well as or instead of catharsis. Good individual work is a co-operative dialogue between the client following your leads, and you following the client's cues. It needs rounding off with affirmative, supportive comment from other group members.

6. Working with content cues. When doing individual cathartic work, you work with content cues - what the person is saying; and with process cues - how they are saying it and what is going in their bodies while they are saying it. This micro-facilitation is at the heart of the co-operative enterprise of 5, individual work. I give here some of the basic techniques for working with content cues. This means working with *what* a person is saying, with their stated difficulty, with meaning, story-line and imagery. For a more detailed account of these, for other techniques, and for a discussion of the issues involved, see my *Six Category Intervention Analysis* (Heron, 1989). In the list below I shall refer to those who are doing the work as 'clients'.

Present tense description. Interrupt analytic talking about a problem, and ask clients to describe - in the present tense as if it is happening now - a specific, traumatic and critical incident, evoking it in literal detail by recall of sights and sounds and smells, of what people said and did.

Psychodrama. As the distress comes to the fore through the use of literal description, invite clients to re-enact the incident as a piece of living theatre, imagining they are in the scene and speaking within it as if it is happening now. Ask them to express fully what was left unsaid at the time, and to say it directly to the central other protagonist in the scene. Catharsis can powerfully occur at this point.

Shifting level. When clients are making a charged statement to the central other protagonist - such as 'I really need you to be here' - in a psychodrama about an incident later in life, you quickly and deftly ask 'Who are you really saying that to?'. They may then very rapidly shift level to a much earlier situation and become, for example, the hurt child speaking to its parent. Often the catharsis dramatically intensifies.

Earliest available memory. Simply ask clients for their earliest available memory of an incident typical of a current difficulty, and work on that with literal description and psychodrama. Depending on how it goes and how early it is, you may get them to shift level inside that psychodrama too.

Scanning. When clients identify a current problem, ask them to scan along the chain of incidents, all of which are linked by the same sort of difficulty and distress. They evoke each scene, then move on to the next, without going into any one event deeply. This loosens up the whole chain.

Slips of the tongue. When a word or phrase slips out that clients didn't intend to say, ask them to repeat it a few times, and to work with the associations and/or process cues. This invariably points the way to some unfinished business.

Contradiction. Ask clients to use words, tone of voice, facial expresson, gesture, posture that lightly and clearly contradict, without qualification, their self-deprecating statements and manner. This interrupts the external invalidation the child within has internalized to keep their distress suppressed, and rapidly opens up into laughter, followed, if you are quick on the cues, by deeper forms of catharsis.

Validation. As the distress comes up, gently and clearly affirm clients, their deep worth, the validity of their pain, their need for release, how much they deserves this time, support and care.

Free attention. If clients are sunk in their distress, ask them to recount some recent pleasant experiences. This will generate some free attention, without which catharsis cannot occur. Go on to the other techniques.

Association. Work with clients' spontaneous, unbidden associations. These include *what is on top* at the start of a session; the sudden surfacing of an earlier memory while working on a later one; the extra bits of recall that come up to illumine a remembered event. The thoughts and insights that arise during a pause in catharsis and as it subsides are important: this re-structuring of awareness is the real fruit, not just the release itself.

Integration of learning. After a major piece of cathartic work that has generated a good deal of insight and re-evaluation, prompt clients to formulate clearly all they have learnt, and to affirm its application to new attitudes of mind, new goals and new behaviours in their life now. At this point cathartic work finds its true *raison d'être.*

7. **Working with process cues.** This means working with *how* clients are talking and being, that is, with tone and charge and volume of voice, with breathing, use of eyes, facial expression, gesture, posture, movement.

Repeating distress-charged words. Ask clients to repeat words and phrases which carry a distressed emphasis, several times, and louder, and perhaps much louder. This will start to discharge the underlying distress, or bring it nearer the surface. This is particularly potent at the heart of a psychodrama, when clients are expressing the hitherto unexpressed to some central other protagonist from their past.

Exaggerating distress-charged movements. Ask the client to repeat and also exaggerate small involuntary agitated movements until they become large and vigorous, then to add the sounds and words that go with them.

This too will start to discharge the underlying distress, or bring it nearer the surface.

Amplifying deepening of the breath. Ask the person who quite suddenly and unawarely breathes in deeply, to continue deep and rapid breathing, making a crescendo of sound on the outbreath. This may release deep sobbing, or screaming and trembling, or a discharge of anger.

Mobilizing distress-locked rigidities. Ask clients to become aware of some bodily rigidity, exaggerate it to let the distress energy pile up in the lock, then to throw the energy out in vigorous movement, finding appropriate sounds and words. So a tight fist and rigid arm is first exaggerated into even greater tension, then converted into rapid thumping on a pillow. You will need to encourage clients not to throttle back the sound, and behind that the long-repressed words.

Acting into. When clients are already feeling the distress and want to discharge it, but are held back by conditioned muscular tension, you suggest they act into the feeling, that is, create a muscular pathway for it, by vigorous pounding and sound for anger, or trembling for fear. If they produce the movement and sound artificially, then often real catharsis will take over.

Physical pressure. When clients are just struggling to get discharge going, or have just started it, or are in the middle of it, you can facilitate release by applying appropriate degrees of pressure to various parts of the body: pressure on the abdomen, midriff or thorax, timed with the outbreath; pressure on the masseter muscle, some of the intercostals, the trapezius, the infraspinatus; pressure on the upper and mid-dorsal vertebrae timed with the outbreath, to deepen the release in sobs; pressure against the soles of the feet and up the legs to precipitate kicking; extending the thoracic spine over the practitioner's knee, timed with the outbreath, to deepen the release of primal grief and screaming; and so on. The pressure is firm and deep, but very sensitively timed to fit and facilitate the cathartic process. Anything ham-fisted and ill-attuned is destructively intrusive.

Physical extension. As clients are moving in and out of the discharge process, you can facilitate the release by gently extending the fingers, if they curl up defensively; or by gently extending the arms; or by drawing the arms out and away from the sides of the body; or by extending an arm while pressing the shoulder back; or by gently raising the head, or uncurling the trunk; and so on. All these extensions are gentle and gradual, so that the client can choose to yield to them and go with them.

Relaxation and light massage. This is an alternative mode of working on physical rigidity. You relax the person and give gentle, caressing massage to rigid areas. Catharsis and/or memory recall may occur as muscle groups give way to the massage.

Physical holding. You reach out lightly to hold and embrace the person at the start, or just before the start, of the release of grief in tears. This can greatly facilitate the intensity of sobbing. Can be combined with aware pressure on the upper dorsal vertebrae at the start of each outbreath. Holding hands at certain points may facilitate discharge. When discharging fear, the person can usefully stand within your embrace, and your fingertips apply light pressure to either side of his or her spine.

Pursuing the eyes. By avoiding eye contact with you, clients are often also at the same time avoiding the distress feelings. You gently pursue their eyes by peering up from under their lowered heads. Re-establishing eye contact may precipitate or continue catharsis.

Regression positions. When process cues suggest either birth or pre-natal material, you can invite clients to assume pre-natal or birth postures, start deep and rapid breathing and wait for the primal experiences to rerun themselves. This may lead into deep and sustained cathartic work in the primal mode. If so, you need to keep leading the person to identify the context, to verbalize insights, and at the end to integrate the learning into his current attitudes and life-style. Regression positions may also be less ambitious like lying in the cot, sitting on the potty, sucking a thumb, etc.

Seeking the context. When clients are deeply immersed in process work and in catharsis, you may judge it fitting to lead them into the associated cognitive mode, asking them to identify and describe the event and its context, to verbalize insights, to make connections with present-time situations and attitudes.

Ending a session. At the end of a cathartic session, it is necessary for you to bring clients back up out of their cathartic regression into present time, by chronological progression at intervals of 5 or 10 years, by affirming positive directions for current living, by describing the immediate environment, by reciting simple lists, by looking forward to the next few days, and so on.

8. Over the shoulder. In a training group for facilitators, when a trainee is practising facilitating the individual work of someone else in the group, you sit a little to the side and behind the trainee, prompting, monitoring and rearranging their interventions. This is a training dialogue in the co-operative mode and needs a deft and light touch.

The feeling dimension: autonomous mode

In this mode you give the group space to manage its own emotional dynamic.

1. Self and peer individual work. Working in pairs, group members take it in turns to be the self-directed client with the other being the facilitator, doing personal growth work on their own internal emotional dynamic. A co-counselling training group is a classic example. This can be done in small groups, with one person the client, and one other (only) the facilitator. All this presupposes there has been training in what to do in both client and facilitator roles.

2. Emotional dynamic peer groups. You set up small peer groups to sit and give each other attention through eye contact, and wait and watch how the group dynamic comes alive, its energy moving about unpredictably and spontaneously, touching different people at different times to cathart, transmute, express, celebrate, or whatever. Work is self-directed, with no-one in the facilitator role.

3. Autonomy lab. This is one of the most powerful ways in which group members can get a feel for managing their own personal dynamic in the context of the dynamic of various sub-groups and of the autonomy lab as a whole. For an account of what goes on in an autonomy lab see 13, the planning dimension, autonomous mode, pages 61-62.

4. No facilitation of feeling phase. You announce a phase in which you will not manage the emotional life the group, but leave members to identify the dynamic and decide whether to stay with it or what process to use to change it.

5. Autonomous monitoring of the emotional dynamic. In this extension of the initiative clause (see 9, planning dimension, autonomous mode, page 60), you have created a climate of shared leadership, in which group members spontaneously identify the emotional dynamic and propose changes in it, alongside your management of this dimension.

6. Trainer-trainee delegation. You appoint one person in the group, or in each of several sub-groups, to manage the emotional dynamic and follow it up with feedback on their facilitation from other members. This is used for training trainers.

7. Charismatic peer groups. You initiate small groups in which each person is equally open to respond in movement, speech, sound and song to the spontaneous promptings of spiritual energy. This differs from 2, in being more intentionally open to altered states of being and awareness.

8. Autonomous expression and celebration. Group members spontaneously express and celebrate in their own way, at their own chosen time.

7. The structuring dimension

The questions here for you, the facilitator, are: how can the group's learning experiences be structured? What form is the learning going to have, and who is going to give it that form? Your concern is with the learning environment, and with experiential methods, structured exercises and their genesis.

Planning and structuring an exercise

The planning and structuring dimensions overlap in the area of structured exercises. Planning interrelates topics, time, resources and learning methods; and methods include exercises. When planning a course you will select certain forms of exercise and give them appropriate places in the programme. The form of an exercise includes its design and the decision-modes used in running it, that is, how it is to be supervised - whether you direct it or the participants manage it on their own.

Planning, then, can include the selection of design and decision-mode for an exercise. It may specify both these aspects of every exercise in great detail, or, at the other extreme, it may give only the barest outline of the forms of exercises to be used at various points in the programme.

The structuring dimension is to do with the immediate and active implementation of the plan. It is at the workface, managing the current learning of these participants at this point in their course. It may give subtantial body to an outline plan. It may modify a detailed plan and adapt it to the evident needs of the learners, or change it radically, or abandon it entirely.

The structuring dimension deals with the existential and situational realities of learning - with what goes on when you are face to face with your learners. It is concerned with giving full working form to the methods of learning. Hence it is under the structuring dimension that I consider in detail the design of exercises and the way the decision-modes can be used in their supervision.

Of course, the planning dimension deals with the course programme as a whole, with the timetabling of topics, resources and all the methods, not just with the structure of exercises. And the structuring dimension is concerned with others ways of giving form to learning as we shall see. However, the nature of the overlap - and of the distinction - between these two dimensions in the area of structured exercises is important to grasp. It is presented in figure 7.1.

	Planning dimension		Structuring dimension
	Place of exercise in course programme	*Design of exercise*	*Supervision of exercise*
Hierarchy: *you alone*			
Co-operation: *you with group*			
Autonomy: *group alone*			

Figure 7.1 *Planning and structuring an exercise*

This diagram shows that the timetabling of an exercise falls under the planning dimension, and the actual supervision of it under the structuring dimension (although the plan may indicate what sort of supervison is to be used). The design of it can fall under either: the plan may include a detailed design of an exercise; or it may indicate that the design is to be worked out at the time, in which case it falls under the structuring dimension. And even a design worked out at the planning stage may have to be modified in the actual learning situation.

The diagram also reminds us that decision-modes used in timetabling an exercise, designing it and supervising it can all be different. You may directively insert into the timetable an exercise the design of which is to be negotiated between you and the group at the time, and which when put into action is to be supervised entirely autonomously by the group.

To say that you have designed an exercise may literally mean that you have *created* it. For convenience, I also take it to mean that you may have *chosen* it from the existing repertoire of exercises in the literature.

Supervision of an exercise and the experiential learning cycle

The supervision of an exercise is about who takes responsibility for what, at different stages of the experiential learning cycle. I reproduce again below, figure 7.2, the diagram of this cycle, as presented in Chapter 4. An exercise which embodies this learning cycle includes several basic stages. Let us suppose the exercise is for the practice of some interpersonal skill, to be done in several small groups. Then the stages are:

1. Modelling the skill. A verbal description is given of the skill, and of what it means to do it well. There may also be a live or video demonstration of this.

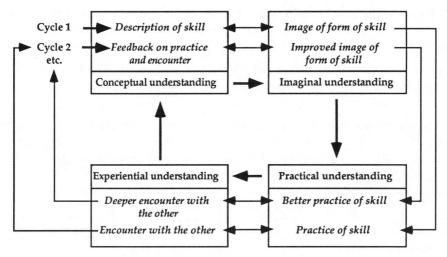

Figure 7.2 *The experiential learning cycle*

2. Describing the exercise. The exercise is designed and instructions are given in detail about its content and procedures: what it is about; the structure and sequence, who does what, the timing of each part. These first two stages are done when everyone is in the large group.

3. Practice. Participants now break into small groups, in which each member takes it in turns to practise the skill.

4. Feedback. In this part of the exercise each person who has taken a turn at practice gives feedback to self, and gets feedback from others, on their performance of the skill. Feedback immediately follows practice.

5. Reruns. The person who has just received feedback reruns the practice to take account of negative feedback, and so to get the skill in better shape. The rerun will again be followed by feedback to self and from the others. There may be two or three reruns.

6. Reflection. This is the part of the exercise in which, when practice and feedback and reruns are finished, small group members reflect on the issues that have arisen.

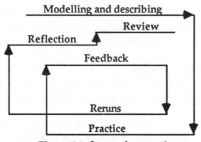

Figure 7.3 *Stages of an exercise*

7. Review. The small groups reconvene in the large group, share some of the issues that arose in the small group reflection phase, review the skill model in the light of practising it, and perhaps also review the exercise design.

Figure 7.3 shows these stages, with reflection and review shown on slightly different levels, since the former occurs in the small groups, and the latter in the whole group.

Now the question is: who is responsible for different parts of this whole procedure? This takes us into the heart of the supervision of learning. I give here, in figure 7.4, a diagram of the whole range of options for who can be responsible for what during the use of an exercise.

Who supervises ➤ the stages of the exercise ↓	Hierarchy: *you alone*	Co-operation: *you with group*	Autonomy: *group alone*
Modelling the skill			
Describing the exercise			
Practice			
Feedback			
Reruns			
Reflection			
Review			

Figure 7.4 *Options for supervising the stages of an exercise*

The bedrock of the exercise is, of course, practice, which is always and necessarily autonomous, in the hands of the learner. I shall return to this diagram under each of the three modes below.

The structuring dimension: hierarchical mode

You take responsibility for structuring the learning process. You control its form. You supervise, directively, the use of the exercises you have devised. You do not actively involve the group in designing the methods, nor do you negotiate changes in the structures which you introduce.

1. Pre-group structuring. You have, of course, complete hierarchical control over the learning environment before the group meets. Here are some of the main issues you will need to consider when preparing to set up the group.

Objectives, programme and methods. What is the group for? How much of the programme will you pre-plan? What methods will you use?

Facilitation and political profile. Will you be alone or will you have a co-facilitator or an assistant facilitator? If so of what gender, and what will their role be? What mix of hierarchy, co-operation and autonomy will you use, and will this change as the group unfolds?

Group composition. Do you have any selection criteria to do with previous experience, education, age, sex, occupation, social class, nationality, psychological well-being, minimum and maximum numbers for the group? Do you need to interview and screen people for the group?

Physical facilities. How many rooms do you need, and of what sort? What sort of furnishings and fittings? Are you in chairs or on cushions? Is the group residential or not? Self-catering or not? In the town or in the country?

Learning resources. What kind of props and equipment do you need to facilitate learning: mattresses, clubs, masks, costumes, musical instruments, records, tapes, slides, CCTV, lights, books, diagrams, articles, photos, films, self-rating questionnaires, paper, paints, crayons, clay, incense, bells, etc?

Fee. How much will you charge? Are there bursaries, and for whom? Or is there a sliding scale? Does the payment that you are taking for yourself properly honour your status and competence?

Advance publicity. Does the brochure or the blurb make it unequivocally clear what the objectives, programme and methods of the group will be, its political profile, who is eligible to join it, who you are, and so on?

Voluntarism. If the group is for some organization, have you checked out whether those attending are freely choosing to attend, or are being sent? Reject any pressure for people to be there.

2. Culture-setting statements. There are here a range of statements that help to establish a certain group culture that will enable learning to flourish. By propounding and recommending them, you are the hierarchical founder of that culture, creating the social structure of learning. They are announced at the outset of the group, with reminders and echoes from time to time after that. When you first announce them, always take time to seek the commitment and assent of group members. Seeking assent takes you toward the co-operative mode; but the primary thrust of this intervention is hierarchical.

Values and objectives. You propose, for example, that the group becomes a place where there is safety and support, vulnerability and fallibility, honesty and risk-taking, liberty and autonomy (voluntary participation), and confidentiality.

You affirm the fundamental value of persons and personhood. You commend worthwhile ways of being which you feel will enable the group to fulfil its objectives of personal growth, skills building, or whatever. You remind people of these objectives and make sure there is full assent to them.

Discipline ground rules. These are simple rules that assist learning by defining clear boundaries of behaviour. They include such things as arriving on time, returning from breaks on time, taking breaks only by group agreement, giving full attention when someone is working in the middle of the group, no smoking/eating/drinking during sessions, no physical violence to person and property, and so on.

Decision-mode ground rules. You make it clear what decision-mode (for choosing what the group does) you are going to use at the outset, and whether and how you may change the decision-mode at later stages of the group. In other words, this is a statement about what you are doing on the planning dimension.

Growth ground rules. You commend a set of behaviours that will intensify personal learning and awareness, and appoint yourself their guardian - which means you point out when someone forgets a rule and invite them to restate what they have said in accordance with the rule. Here is one typical set, for a personal growth oriented group:

1. Speak in the first person singular - 'I' instead of 'one' or 'we' or 'you' - in order to own fully what is being said.

2. Address others in the second person - 'you' instead of 'her' or 'him' or 'they' - in order to encounter them fully and directly.

3. Take risks in amplifying and disclosing what is going on inside you when it is going on, and be open to others doing the same, in order to learn more about yourself and others.

4. Try to find the statement about your own experience that lies behind the question directed at someone else's experience: in this way you can become more aware of your own concerns.

5. Try to spot and interrupt the defence of unawarely dumping and displacing your distress on others: in order to own your distress, work on it, and free yourself from it.

3. The direction of exercises. You design, supervise the introduction and use of a structured exercise as a means of experiential learning. Once active within the exercise, group members are, of course, autonomous, self-directed in their learning. But the form of the exercise, and overall supervision of it, are determined by you - in the hierarchical mode.

The learner has the security of your hierarchical direction together with plenty of scope for autonomous practice within this structure. This is a powerful combination in early stages of skills-building and personal growth.

Experiential learning cycle. With each exercise, you take people through this cycle, fundamental for learning. The seven steps of the procedure given earlier in this chapter can conveniently be reduced to three:

1. A clear statement from you of the rationale of the exercise, the conceptual model behind it, followed by a clear account of how to do the exercise, its time structure, the use of feedback, rerunning and reflection.

2. People do the exercise, usually in small groups, with some time for the action, some time for feedback (from self first and then from peers), some time for rerunning the action, if appropriate, and some time for reflection on the issues.

3. People come together with you in the whole group, for an exchange of reflection between the small groups, and for review with you of the conceptual model you presented at the outset.

You are the hierarch in designing the exercise and taking people through the first two stages. Thereafter, the decision-mode of supervision changes. Stage 2 gives great scope for autonomous practice and feedback, and stage 3 is a cooperative review with you. See figure 7.5.

Who supervises ➡ the stages of the exercise ⬎	Hierarchy: *you alone*	Co-operation: *you with group*	Autonomy: *group alone*
Modelling the skill	X		
Describing the exercise	X		
Practice			X
Feedback			X
Reruns			X
Reflection			X
Review		X	

Figure 7.5 *Two hierarchical stages in supervision of an exercise*

If you go round the small groups and make your contribution during feedback, reruns, practice and reflection, then the above table will also have Xs in the co-operation column on each of these four rows. If you are contributing to a rerun, this means either that you propose it, or give some of the feedback after it.

Procedural ground-rules. These help to amplify and clarify stage 2 above - autonomous practice and feedback. They maximize learning within the exercise. Two classic ones in skills-building exercises are:

1. Practice should always be followed by feedback. The best order of feedback in a role play is from protagonist to self, from the other role players to protagonist, finally from observers to protagonist, followed by discussion.

2. The protagonist should wherever possible rerun behaviours that are off track, until he or she gets them on track and knows what this feels like.

Uses of exercises. Their overall use is as a method of experiential learning, which includes personal growth and all kinds of personal and professional skills in handling oneself and others. They may be used as a learning sequence in the overall programme, and in an impromptu way to relate to a live issue that emerges for one or more persons in the group. They can also uses in relation to the stages of a group and its emotional dynamic:

1. To start a new group - to break the ice, get-to-know-you, loosen defences, reduce anxiety, clarify expectations, define needs.

2. To end a group - to review learning, plan transfer of learning to the outside world, deal with unfinished business, share appreciations, deal with separation anxiety, say farewell.

3. To open and close each day or session in an ongoing group: a ritual coming together for, and departure from, the shared learning.

4. To transform the emotional dynamic: see 4, the feeling dimension, hierarchical mode, page 95.

It is also important to remember that the term 'exercise' as used here includes ritual and all kinds of charismatic and transpersonal structured experiences; and all kinds of expressive and celebratory structures. Learning is as wide as living.

The focus of exercises. Exercises can be used to structure the following: discussion within the group; decision-making within the group; encounter between people within the group; conflict resolution within the group; group process analysis; creativity and problem-solving; expressive skills; aesthetic skills; technical skills (e.g. clinical, mechanical, financial, etc.); management and organizational skills; interactive skills for personal and professional life; assertiveness skills; social change skills; personal and transpersonal growth.

Personal and transpersonal growth may include: sensory awareness, breathing and body work, primal and general regression, monodrama, psychodrama and role play, re-evaluation and reintegration, guided fantasy and active imagination, attitude and belief-system restructuring, creative expression and celebration, goal-setting and life-planning, psychic awareness and energy work, sublimation and transmutation, ritual, meditation and charismatic work. Many of these items overlap.

The content of exercises. They can be about imaginary situations, either on the job or off the job, and either typical or bizarre and extreme. Alternatively, they can be about real situations, here and now in the group, from someone's past experience, or from someone's expected future experience. All of these, except here and now experience in the group, will involve the use of role play: one person in the central role practising some skill or exploring some experience, with other group members in supporting roles.

4. Total, or partial, directive supervision. All the structured exercises used may be designed and managed by you, or only some of them may be: others being designed and managed co-operatively with you or autonomously by the group. As you proceed through the history of a skills training group, you may include more and more co-operative, then autonomous, supervision.

5. Autocratic, or consultative, directive supervision. When introducing a structured exercise as in 3 above - modelling the skill and explaining the format - you may do this *autocratically*, without eliciting views from the group, and either with or without a supporting rationale. This is often best for beginners.

You may introduce the exercise *consultatively*, in which case you elicit views from the group on the modelling and the format, but you may or may not take these into account when giving your final directions.

When being consultative, you can be either *facilitator-centred* and present your own ideas before theirs, or *group-centred* and ask participants to share their ideas before yours; but in either case you make the concluding decision about the exercise.

As trainee skill increases, the more appropriate it is to move from autocratic to consultative forms of directive supervision, and then at later stages to co-operative and autonomous supervision.

6. Directive choice of decision-modes for supervision. You make a directive decision, autocratic or consultative, about what decision-modes to use in the supervision of learning exercises - whether they shall be hierarchical, co-operative or autonomous, in what combinations and at what points in the procedure. This is a higher-level decision and comes before any of the previous entries on supervision. It, in turn, is preceded by 7, following.

7. Decision-mode mastery for design and supervision of structures. As hierarchical facilitator, you need a clear grasp of all the different decision-modes and the various ways they can be applied to the process of learning by structured exercises. Figure 7.4 on page 106 shows the options.

8. Directive choice of decision-procedures. You make a directive decision, autocratic or consultative, about what decision-procedures to use when in the co-operative mode. For a reminder about the difference between decision-modes and decision-procedures, see Chapter 3, page 48.

9. Unilateral review of structuring. On your own, you review the design of exercises, the sorts and uses of them, decision-modes and decision-procedures used in supervision. This may lead you to restructure some of these things.

The structuring dimension: co-operative mode

You structure the learning methods *with* the group, co-operating with them in devising how the learning shall proceeed. So group members participate with you in modelling the skill to be practised, in designing the content and procedure of structured exercises, and in supervising the running of them.

This co-operative approach between you and the group is appropriate for those who are in an advanced stage of learning, or who have a lot of professional experience in the field to which the learning applies.

It enables group member directly to relate the training exercises to their personal learning needs and goals, and to job-related situations and difficulties. At the same time, they can do this with guidance and assistance from you.

When no exercises are being used, your facilitation interacts with what people are saying and doing, so that the process is like an enabling dialogue. This relatively unstructured approach is appropriate for any stage of learning

The first intervention below sets the scene for all subsequent activities. Group members participate with you in defining the ethos of learning.

1. Culture-setting contract. Instead of making culture-setting statements and creating the culture unilaterally, as in the hierarchical mode, you work co-operatively with the group, eliciting from them their proposals for values and ground-rules, sharing your own views, and negotiating a final contract. You may need to prompt the the group about possible values, about the different sorts of ground-rules - discipline, decision and growth - and of options within these; but the group is as active as you in defining and giving shape to the culture. For a reminder of the full range of culture-setting statements see 2, under the hierarchical mode, pages 107-108.

2. Co-operation on tailor-made exercises. The group - or one or more members of it - participate with you in structuring the learning. Within this co-operative decision-mode it is probably best to use the decision-procedure of consensus.

If the exercise is to practise some skill, the group participate with you in creating a model of what good practice is.

You discuss the design of an exercise - the content of it and the procedures in running it - with those who are going to use it: they co-operate with you in modifying and shaping it until you all agree it may best meet their needs. In this way it can be tailor-made to fit their particular weaknesses and strengths, or the special circumstances of their work or life.

The group co-operate with you in the final review stage, distilling learning out of the practice and reconsidering the original model of the skill in the light of all this. So figure 7.4 now becomes figure 7.6 below.

Who supervises ──▶ the stages of the exercise ──┐	Hierarchy: *you alone*	Co-operation: *you with group*	Autonomy: *group alone*
Modelling the skill		X	
Describing the exercise		X	
Practice			X
Feedback			X
Reruns			X
Reflection			X
Review		X	

Figure 7.6 *Co-operative stages in supervision of an exercise*

If you go round the small groups and make your contribution during feedback, reruns, practice and reflection, then the above table will also have Xs in the co-operation column on each of these four rows. If you are contributing to a rerun, this means that you propose it or give some of the feedback after it. Another modification is when you are hierarchical about modelling, and co-operative in designing and describing the exercise.

3. Total, or partial, co-operative supervision. All structured exercises used may be designed and/or supervised co-operatively, or only some of them may be: others being designed and supervised hierarchically by you or autonomously by the group. As a skills training group proceeds, you may include more and more co-operative, then autonomous, supervision.

4. Negotiated, or co-ordinated, supervision. When co-operating with group members about designing and managing exercises, in 2 above, you can either *negotiate* with them, or *co-ordinate* their thinking and decision-making. If you negotiate, you can be *facilitator-centred* and put your own ideas forward first, or you can be *group-centred* and invite participants to make their proposals before yours. And with any of these options, you will need to choose a decision-procedure: informal consensus will probably work best. All the basic distinctions made in 3, 4, 5 and 9, in relation to the planning dimension, co-operative mode, pages 55-56, apply here also. A brief visual reminder is shown below in figure 7.7.

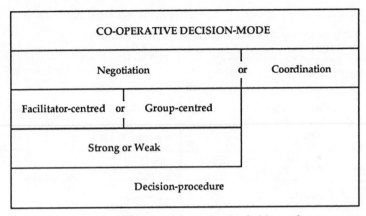

Figure 7.7 *Elements of the co-operative decision-mode*

5. Co-operative choice of decision-modes for supervision. Here you make a co-operative decision with the group, by negotiation or co-ordination, about what decision-modes to use in the supervision of learning exercises - whether they shall be hierarchical, co-operative or autonomous, in what combinations and at what points in the procedure.

6. Co-operative choice of decision-procedures. You make a co-operative decision, by negotiation or co-ordination, about what decision-procedures to use within co-operative supervision. Often it is artificial and excessively formalistic to go to these lengths: informal consensus is the tacit choice.

7. Co-operative review of structuring. You and the group take time out to review the structure of the learning that has gone on: the design of exercises, the sorts and uses of them, the use of decision-modes and decision-procedures. This may lead to various kinds of restructuring. The item overlaps with programme review, 7, within the planning dimension, co-operative mode.

8. *Ad hoc* co-operative supervision. You are called in while a small group is busy with autonomous practice, to help out with some problem. Or you have already agreed with the group that you will go round visiting all the small practice groups in turn, contributing to feedback, reruns, practice and reflection.

9. Process structuring. The ongoing process of an unstructured group is influenced, shaped and given special forms by your interventions - which elicit, interpret and confront. In this you co-operate, like a midwife, with the emerging behaviour of the group, creating a richer and deeper learning experience.

There are no given exercises here: the group is unstructured in that sense, as is the T-group, encounter group or therapy group. But what people say and do becomes more authentic and open by virtue of your midwifery.

I reproduce here from my *Six Category Intervention Analysis*, (Heron, 1989), a bedrock range of facilitator interventions. They are all very simple and go together as a set of everyday working tools. Their purpose is to unfold group members' self-discovery, and to do so with minimal input from you. They enable you, if you use them well, to be highly effective while maintaining a low profile. So here is the *facilitator's tool-kit*.

Be here now. This is the everyday mystical one. You are centred, present, with your awareness unencumbered, in the moment that is now. This has nothing to do with what you are saying or your social behaviour, it's all to do with how you are being. You are not distracted by the concerns of the past or future. You are fully aware of the present, but not caught up in or anxiously engaged with it. You are intensely in the moment, and yet not at all of it.

Some simple bodily adjustments can aid entry into this state: you can relax your breathing and deepen it a bit; you can let go of all unnecessary muscular tension in your posture and find one that feels both comfortable and attentive. But the state is not to do with your body, it is to do with inner alertness. To use a metaphor, you are awake to the moment, not distractedly dreaming it.

Be there now. The previous state seems to me to be a pre-condition of all effective catalytic behaviours. One reason for this concerns the mystical principle of the identity of the centre of being with the circumference of being. So to be here now is very much also to be there now. When you are attuned to your own centre, you are already very open to the reality of others. Within the 'I' is found the 'Thou'.

Giving free attention. This is the extension from being here now within the self, to being there now with the other. When you are here now, you have abundant free attention, which is not enslaved by past, present or future content, and which can dwell with and energize your group.

This is a subtle and intense activity of your consciousness mediated by gaze, posture, facial expression, sometimes touch. It has the qualities of being supportive of the essential being and worth of group members independent of anything they say or do; of being expectant, waiting for the potential fulness of human beings to emerge in ways that are meaningful to them and their fulfilment; and of being wider and deeper than the content of their speech, encompassing all their body cues, their whole individual way of being and doing, their total living reality. It's also relaxed, a little laid back and benign.

Simple echoing. You echo back the last word, or the last few words, a person said before pausing. The words are echoed back just as stated, or perhaps slightly rephrased, and without any interrogative inflection (i.e. not as an indirect question), and without any inflection that carries judgment or value-loading. Simple echoing is a way of conveying to people attention, interest, and above all an invitation to develop the theme in any way that is meaningful to them. So they can go on talking on their own chosen path, whereas any question, however open, leads off in a certain direction.

Selective echoing. You are listening very fully and with fine tuning to everything a person is saying. You then reflect or echo back something not at the end but from the middle of the speech, some word or phrase that carries an emotional charge or stands out as significant in its context. Again there is no interrogative inflection or any other kind of inflection on your echo. This gives space for people, if they wish (they may not), to explore more fully and in any chosen direction the hidden implications of the reflected word or phrase. Selective echoing is usually used to follow the speaker deeper into territory already entered. But it can be used to echo something that leads into new territory.

Open questions and closed questions. Here is a simple but central polar pair of interventions. The open question does not have one right answer, but gives plenty of space for the group member to come up with several possible answers, e.g., 'What do you remember about your first school?' The closed question only has one answer, the right one, e.g., 'What was the name of your first school?' The distinction between open and closed is not an absolute one. Some questions are ambiguous, e.g., 'Do you believe in school?' may be heard as open or closed. And there are degrees of openness(or closure), e.g., 'What do you remember about your first school?' is more open than 'What do you remember about the headmistress of your first school?'

In general, open questions tend to be more eliciting than closed questions simply because they give more scope for self-directed exploration and discovery. But there is no hard and fast rule: it depends on the context and the timing. In any case, the skilled facilitator can ask both open and closed questions as and when appropriate, and can control the degree of openness on open questions.

Highly anxious facilitators, compulsive helpers, often have difficulty with mastering open questions: their anxiety contracts their questioning into the closed form. Hence they may have anxious participants worrying about whether they dare give an answer in case they get it wrong.

Questions, whether open or closed, need to be participant-centred and tuned in to the participant's reality, rather than facilitator-centred and deriving from your curiosity or determination to be proved right, etc.

There are three final points. Questions can be balanced between *following* and *leading*. They can be asked of one person, or of the whole group. They also give you the opportunity to be confronting and consciousness-raising, as well as purely eliciting.

Empathic divining. When a group member says something that has an implicit feeling, thought or intention which is lurking between the lines and which is not fully expressed, you divine this unstated content and put it back to them. So if someone says, in a certain context, and with a certain kind of tone and inflection, 'I can't say any more', then you may say 'It seems as though you are quite frightened'. You are divining that part of the speaker's attitude of mind that is just below the surface of what is being said, and that is affecting how it is being said. It may be a feeling, a belief or an intention, or some mixture of these. You will pick it up mainly - within a given context - from the form of words and the tone of voice, aided perhaps by facial and other bodily cues. You express it always as a statement, never as a question, with an opening such as 'It sounds/seems as though you...'. You can also use it when a person is not speaking, but full of facial cues; then you say 'It looks/seems as though you...'.

This intervention often needs a little practice before people get it right. It is a very precise test of empathy. The key to success is only to divine what is actually emerging between the lines. Sometimes you may put back something that goes way down below any lurking content, and this throws the speaker in too deep too soon. Sometimes you may 'divine' your own projected agenda.

Empathic divining overlaps with giving an attributive *interpretation* (see meaning dimension, hierarchical mode, 5 on page 64). But the latter can go beyond empathic divining and penetrate to something that is hidden by the lines, not just showing through them.

Empathic divining can also be used with *confronting* intent and effect, to raise consciousness in people about some emerging attitude which they are defensively trying not to acknowledge. When applied to distress-charged statements and distress-charged facial and other bodily cues, it may also be used with *cathartic* effect, bringing the distress further up toward, or even into, discharge.

Empathic divining may also be applied to the group process as a whole, in which case it is based on the verbal and non-verbal cues of several group members over a recent time-period. It then states some as yet unidentified issue which is starting to emerge through the group dynamic. Your intent may simply be to *elicit*, or it may also be to *confront*.

Checking for understanding. This intervention, a special case of empathic divination, is only used when someone, groping for words, says something confused or contradictory. You try to divine what they want to say, tidy up their statement to express this clearly, and put it back to them with the preface, 'Let me see, are you saying that...?' Then they can either agree; or disagree, clarify what they meant, and get back on a more coherent course.

The intervention can also be used for some dialogue or group discussion which lacks coherence: you pick out from the confused exchange what might be the primary issue and relevant points. You put this back to the group as a whole, and seek clarification from anyone in the group, not only those involved in the talk.

Paraphrasing. You rephrase in your own words something important which a participant has expressed. This manifests solidarity, shows you are really listening and understanding. And it gives people a chance to check their formulation against yours, and so find out if they have said what they really wanted to say. This is on a smaller scale than logical marshalling, which is next.

Logical marshalling. Whereas empathic divining deals with what is sensed between the lines, logical marshalling deals with what is on the lines of what group members have been saying. You organize the explicit content of a whole chapter of the discussion, summarize it, maybe interrelate parts of it, maybe indicate directions in which it seems to be leading, and put all this back succinctly to the group. This may prompt

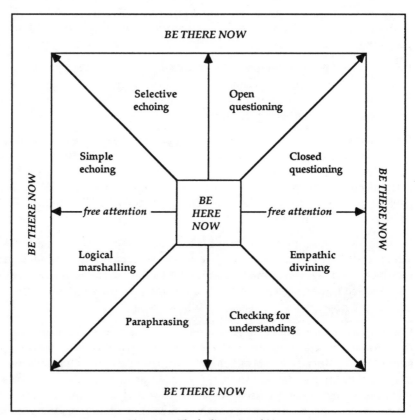

Figure 7.8 *The facilitator's tool-kit*

members to review and revise their train of thought and feeling; or it may provide a springboard for launching off in some new direction.

The above eleven items can be set out in a simple diagram which represents the *facilitator's tool-kit*, as in figure 7.8 above.

All the tools can be used for *eliciting*. Empathic divining overlaps with *interpreting*, and can be used for *confronting* and for moving toward *catharsis*. Questioning can also be used for *confronting*. Both questioning and divining can focus on facial and other bodily cues, when a person is not speaking, as well as on content and mode of speech.

The tool-kit is a box made up of four smaller boxes, each of which is divided diagonally into two compartments, for two related interventions of the same basic sort. It is useful, if you are a beginner, to have a copy of this diagram near you when working with a group, to remind yourself of the basic range of options available to you.

Following, consulting, proposing or leading. When it comes to opening up new territory for the group, there are four options:

1. Participants have already started to enter it and you follow;

2. You consult group members and ask them where they want to go next, maybe referring back to items on an agenda agreed earlier - if there is a consensus about where to go, that's where you all go;

3. You propose a change of area and seek participants' assent;

4. You simply lead the group into new territory.

When proposing a shift or leading into it, you do so because you divine it as seeking to emerge; because you see it as appropriate to fulfil a balanced programme; because there is a contract to cover it; or because it has been left unfinished from an earlier session. The flexible practitioner will be able to use all these four as and when appropriate.

Working with non-verbal cues. There are important cues evident in the facial expression and body language of group members who are not speaking. There are five basic kinds. Whatever else is going on, it is essential to scan the whole group with your eyes at regular intervals so that you can spot these cues and work with them as appropriate.

Picking up on pensive cues. You ask the open question 'What are you thinking?' of a group member who has that typical brief reflective facial expression, indicative of an inner reaction to what other people in the group are saying. The person may not verbalize the thoughts unless asked; but when expressed they often enrich the interaction. 'What are you thinking?' is an open question rather than a closed one. There is no single right answer. The pensive person's presenting thought is usually at the leading edge of a whole cluster of related thoughts.

Picking up on wanting-to-speak cues. You put an open question such as 'What is your view?' to someone whose facial and other movements show that they want to say something. Or eye contact and bringing in the person with a hand gesture and saying their name, will be sufficient.

Picking up on feeling cues. These cues may combine with pensive cues, or wanting-to-speak cues, or may be evident on their own. They show shock, surprise, delight, loving care, irritation, impatience, anxiety, and so on. You can use empathic divining, 'It looks as though you...'; or open questioning, 'How are you feeling?' Again, the presenting feeling may well have other, sometimes quite different, facets.

Picking up on cathartic cues. This is a special case of the previous entry. The eyes, facial expression, other bodily cues, show that distress emotion is coming up, moving toward discharge. The fists are clenched (anger); the lips and jaw are trembling (fear); the eyes are filling with tears (grief); laughter is about to break out (embarrassment). Empathic divining may bring the distress a little nearer identification, ownership, acceptance and release. So for filling eyes you may say 'It looks as though you're holding on to so much hurt and pain'. For sustained discharge, of course, you will move over into full-blown cathartic interventions.

Picking up on alienation cues. The facial expression and perhaps the posture show that a group member is alienated, has mentally and emotionally cut out of the group, and is sunk in their own internal process. You can use empathic divining and say 'It looks as though you...'. Or you can gently ask an open question: 'What is going on for you right now?'

Bring in, draw out, shut out. You scan the group regularly with your eyes to pick up on non-verbal cues among those who are not talking. From these, you can *bring in* one person by eye contact, hand gesture, questioning, divining. You can *draw out* someone who is already talking by eye contact, hand gesture, echoing, questioning, divining, checking for understanding, paraphrasing, marshalling. You can *shut out* someone who is talking, with a deft gesture from one hand, while simultaneously *bringing in* someone else with your other hand: you can do this without any words, like a *traffic cop*. Or you can also add words - and question, divine, check for understanding, paraphrase or marshal what the current speaker has just said, and put this to someone else for comment. Thus you keep a low profile while effectively managing contribution-rates, eliciting self-discovery and interpersonal learning in the group. Figure 7.9 shows the options.

In the top box on the left of this diagram, there are those elements of behaviour that underly the use of the ten further items. *Being present* means *being here now, being there now* and *giving free attention,* as I have described these on page 115. *Scanning* means continuously looking round the group to pick up non-verbal cues of the five kinds given on pages 119-120. *Timing* means making your intervention deftly, surely and without inappropriate time-lag. *Choice of words* refers to the diction and also to the grammatical form of verbal interventions. *Paralinguistics* refer to your manner of speech and include: emotional tone of voice; volume and pitch of sound; rhythm and rate of speech; use of inflection and emphasis; use of pauses and silence. *Body language* covers your use of relative position, touch, posture, facial expression, gesture and eye contact.

Relative position is a potent feature of facilitation: where you sit or stand in relation to the whole group or to one person with whom you are working; when and how you move from one position to another.

In the list of ten interventions, the first two are non-verbal - eye contact and gesture. These are the two non-verbal behaviours most used in controlling contribution rates and managing interaction in a group. *Traffic cop* refers to simultaneous hand gestures: one hand is held up to shut out the current speaker, the other hand is beckoning to bring in someone else.

	BRING IN	DRAW OUT	SHUT OUT
Being present SCANNING Timing Choice of words Paralinguistics Body language			
Eye contact			
Gesture: traffic cop			
Simple echoing			
Selective echoing			
Open questioning			
Closed questioning			
Empathic divining			
Checking for underst.			
Paraphrasing			
Logical marshalling			

Figure 7.9 *Managing contribution rates*

10. Elicit-inform gradient. When you are facilitating the group in a reflection or review phase, in open discussion, you may want to agree with, or disagree with and correct, what group members say; and to impart further information. This is also the group seminar or tutorial situation. You then need the elicit-inform gradient, shown in figure 7.10.

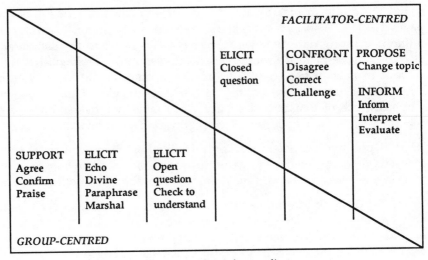

Figure 7.10 *Elicit-inform gradient*

It includes the facilitator's tool-kit, given in 9 above, together with several other verbal interventions. The eight *eliciting* interventions of the tool-kit are included in the second, third and fourth columns in figure 7.10. To these are added *supportive* interventions on the group-centred side, and *confronting, proposing* and *informing* ones on the facilitator-centred side. The items given under each of these further categories are self-explanatory. You could also add, alongside supportive interventions at the group-centred end, *cathartic* interventions, in the form of releasing tension through laughter. Be group-centred earlier on and facilitator-centred later on.

The structuring dimension: autonomous mode

You give space for group members to devise their own forms of learning, and to manage the process by themselves. *This is the heartland of autonomous learning.* Participants are not only being self-directed in practice, but they are also being self-directed in managing the process of learning: they are creating and supervising the structures and procedures that mediate their learning.

1. Autonomous design and supervision of structures. Where there is skills-building or growth work in small groups, you delegate to each group the design and supervision of whatever structures it uses. Small group members confer about the design to meet their special learning needs and goals. There are different kinds and degrees of delegation here.

Contractual delegation. The contract you make with the group may cover time and general learning objectives only, and everything else is delegated. Members practise, for a given period, any skill they choose, in terms of any exercises and forms of peer supervision they devise. Or the contract may cover time and a specific learning objective - to practise a particular skill - and the choice of exercise and the way of supervising it are delegated. Or the contract may specify the time, the skill and the main method such as role play - and everything beyond that is delegated.

The contract can allocate modelling the skill, designing the exercise and supervision of it in all sorts of different ways to different combinations of: delegation to the group, collaboration with you, and direction by you.

Functional delegation. You delegate different design and supervision functions to different people in the small group. Some people are to create the model of good practice, others are to design content (what the exercise is about), others are to design procedure (how the exercise is done), and yet others are to devise forms of peer supervision of the exercise. You also delegate a process whereby these three sub-groups can integrate their work. Functional delegation presupposes some form of contractual delegation about time, learning objectives, kind of exercise to be used.

For full-blown delegation, the supervisory table now appears as in figure 7.11, the only co-operation with you being in the final review phase.

Who supervises the stages of the exercise	Hierarchy: *you alone*	Co-operation: *you with group*	Autonomy: *group alone*
Modelling the skill			X
Describing the exercise			X
Practice			X
Feedback			X
Reruns			X
Reflection			X
Review		X	

Figure 7.11 *Autonomous stages in supervision of an exercise*

The above table shows very complete delegation. It could be much more piecemeal and limited, with Xs in some of the other rows and columns.

2. Total, or partial, delegation of design and supervision. All the structured exercises used may be designed and/or supervised autonomously, or only some of them may be: others being designed and supervised hierarchically by you or co-operatively by you and the group.

3. Autonomous choice of decision-modes for supervision. Group members decide on their own what decision-modes to use in the design and supervision of learning exercises - whether, *amongst themselves*, they shall be hierarchical, co-operative or autonomous, in what combinations and at what points in the procedure. This item could also refer to a group which chooses to bring you (or some other facilitator) back in to be hierarchical or co-operative.

4. Autonomous choice of decision-procedures. Group members decide on their own what decision-procedures to use when cooperating together within autonomous design and supervision of learning.

5. Autonomous review of structuring. Group members on their own take time out to review the structure of the learning that has gone on: the design of exercises, the sorts and uses of them, the use of decision-modes and decision-procedures. This may lead to various kinds of restructuring. It overlaps with autonomous progamme review, see 7, planning dimension, autonomous mode, page 60.

6. No facilitation of structures phase. You announce a phase in which you will not offer structures or exercises, but leave group members to devise these among themselves. You may, of course, still be active on other dimensions.

7. Autonomous monitoring of structuring. In this extension of the initiative clause (see 9, autonomous mode, planning dimension, page 60), you have created a climate of shared leadership, in which group members spontaneously propose ways of structuring their learning - independent of and alongside your management of this dimension.

8. Trainer-trainee delegation. You delegate the role of devising and also facilitating structures to a group member for a period, in the whole group or in training sub-groups, followed by feedback to that person. Both this and the previous strategy presuppose that the group will have received some kind of training in presenting and working with structured exercises, or with process structuring.

9. Autonomous projects. You delegate to small groups the task of working on their own on a project of their own choice, consistent with the overall objectives of the course. This is a project other than skills building and so does not fall under the previous analysis of design and supervision of structures. It goes with 3, planning dimension, autonomous mode, page 59.

10. Self-directed client. In personal growth work, participants choose what methods to use, whether psychodrama, body work, transpersonal work, and so on; and also direct themselves in the use of the method. This is the approach in co-counselling when the client opts for a free attention only contract. It can be used in any context to help internalize skill in method. This is one-to-one delegation.

11. Facilitator as self-directed client. You take time in the group for your own development and learning, setting up a structure to meet your own needs for growth and change. As an exemplary *member* of the group, you motivate risk-taking and initiative in others.

12. Autonomy lab. You set up a whole workshop, or a major part of a workshop, as an autonomous learning environment. You explain the model and invite group members to contract into it. Inside the lab, the group is leaderless. The learning resources of the lab are the group members themselves with their particular skills and experiences, physical resources such as books, articles, tapes, CCTV, etc., and yourself. You only do anything when asked by one or more participants to meet some specific learning need.

Group members exercise total initiative and autonomy in deciding what their learning needs are, how to meet them, in what order and with whom. Everyone has the challenge of structuring their own learning experience, pacing and changing it, through negotiation with others. A useful instruction before the lab is to invite each person to prepare a list of what they want to get from or with others, and what they have to offer to others. The lab starts with all these lists posted up. When not being called upon as a resource, you go around meeting your own learning needs. See also pages 61-62.

13. Leaderless group. The only way in which a group can be totally autonomous in forming its own learning environment, is if you encourage it to come into being as a leaderless peer group, from which of course you are absent. To the extent that you advise the group in advance about values, ground rules, experiential exercises, you give it a hierarchical impulse.

8. The valuing dimension

On this dimension, you are seeking to create a climate of respect for persons and personal autonomy, in which group members feel valued and honoured, so that they can become more authentic, disclosing their true needs and interests, finding their integrity, determining their own reality and humanity.

The person

By a person, I mean the soul manifesting in alert, aware action: a being celebrating their self-determination in conscious deeds. A person emerges through their expressed intentions. 'I choose, and become a distinct person.' Through electing to do something the potential person becomes actual.

Hence the person is a self-creating being. The sum total of my past acts constitutes the person I have become today. Within limits set by the fields of influence to which the everyday self is open, I am shaping my personality, making myself through my daily choices.

The person is a seamless whole, an interacting system which in simplified form has four psychological modes of being: *willing* is the diamond apex whose facets are cut by the aware discrimination of *thinking,* which is made wise by the holistic receptivity of *intuition,* and grounded in the participation in being of *feeling.* This is shown as a pyramid in figure 8.1.

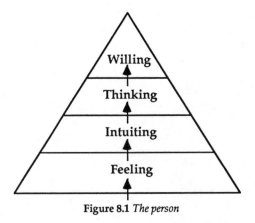

Figure 8.1 *The person*

The pyramid, as arrowhead, is pointing towards deeds: the four psychological modes converge upon enterprise and endeavour. From our felt participation in the world, we open intuitively to grasp a total situation, then discriminate thoughtfully in order to act within it. This corresponds with the manifold, epistemological learning pyramid, Chapter 1, page 13.

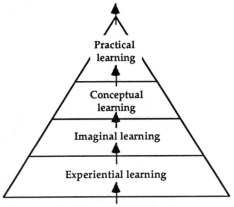

Figure 8.2 *Manifold learning*

A person, through the manifold of learning - shown again in figure 8.2 - encounters the world (experiential learning), identifies patterns of form and process in it (imaginal learning), which is the basis for the development of language and knowledge (conceptual learning), and this is applied in a wide range of skills (practical learning). Some skills are acquired in infancy before the mastery of language, but the vast majority of human skills develop in the context of linguistic competence.

This basic thrust of human learning, from encounter with the world, through imaginal grasp and reflection, to action in the world, has superimposed upon it another dynamic, when persons make their learning more intentional by using the experiential learning cycle, as described in Chapter 4. The four stages of this cycle make another sequence, a continuous self-generated loop, through the basic learning pyramid, as in figure 8.3.

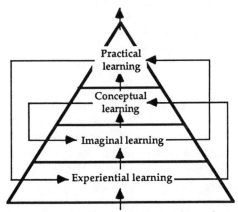

Figure 8.3 *The experiential learning cycle*

This cycle is not just for learning in some group. It is for autonomous living too - the person living as a self-creating being. But autonomy and the creation of personality, through living this learning cycle, clearly admit of degrees. There are many different states of personhood from those in which it is largely potential to those in which it is actualized in many ways.

States of personhood

The behaviour of a deranged and deluded person may be unawarely pushed around by all kinds of forces, yet it may still exhibit little areas where minimal self-determination is exercised. To refer to someone like this as a 'person' is both to affirm those areas and the individual's capacity for increasing the range of self-determined behaviour. Such a one is in reality more a potential person than an actual one. It follows that personhood, manifest in any full sense, is an achievement.

In truth, there are as many different mixes of potential and actual personhood as there are people, in this world and in other dimensions of being. But certain broad types of mix can usefully be identified, as follows. In the first three below, the autonomous person is more embryonic than actual, although less so as we go through them.

1. The deranged person. Behaviour is erratically and chaotically subject to psychic, psychosocial and physical influences, into which the person has little or no insight and over which they have little or no control. They do not see that their autonomy is being buried by the invasion. Voluntary choice is minimal and severely restricted.

2. The compulsive person. Behaviour is in certain ways rigid, maladaptive, repetitive and relatively unaware. The person can see that their autonomy is oppressed by these restricted ways of being, but has little insight into their origins or into how to get rid of them. Most of us are compulsive in some areas of our behaviour, slipping in and out of distress-driven victim, oppressor, rescuer and rebel roles. The problem lies in buried, out-of-date mechanisms of emotional survival, and the repressed early pain, discussed in Chapter 2. In non-compulsive areas there may be greater or lesser scope for voluntary choice, real autonomy, depending on the degree of the next item.

3. The conventional person. Behaviour unreflectively conforms to the prevailing norms of the wider culture, and of the smaller social groups within it, to which the person belongs. The person may have some, little or no awareness that such conformity constrains really autonomous behaviour; but the more conscious they are of the hindrance, so much the less is their compliance unreflective. Furthermore, the person may be conventional in some areas of behaviour while autonomous in others. And finally, a person may convert conventional behaviour into autonomous behaviour without changing its external form, because the person can see the point of it and can make it their own.

Deranged behaviour is the extreme of compulsive behaviour but without the compulsive person's awareness that it limits autonomy. Deranged behaviour is too unaware to conform to convention; it is sub-conventional.

Some compulsive behaviour is also conventional behaviour, since some conventions are compulsions writ large as social norms. Other compulsive behaviour is non-conventional but tolerated, such as drunkenness within limits. And yet other compulsive behaviour is unconventional, and may further be regarded as deviant or anti-social.

Much conventional behaviour is non-compulsive, and this is what I include under 3 above. Either it is a matter of intelligent social coherence, even though people adhere to it through unreflective conformity; or it has symbolic significance as a form of the culture; or it is an arbitrary social practice, based perhaps on some mixture of ignorance and custom.

In the second group of different mixes of potential and actual personhood, autonomy is no longer embryonic - it is born. The person is more actual than potential: significant voluntary choice is now being exercised. But there are increasing degrees of freedom and self-determination, of the emergence of the person, involved in the following group.

4. The creative person. Behaviour is genuinely autonomous in some major areas of human endeavour: parenthood and the family; friendship, relationship and intimacy; education; social and political action; the professions; the arts; the sciences and the humanities; economics, commerce and industry; agriculture; and so on. The person has values, norms and beliefs to which they are internally committed, and to which they give systematic, creative expression in one or more of these domains of action. Their choices transcend unreflective conformity to the prevailing beliefs, norms and values of these domains. The creative person changes their own behaviour only in so far as it is part of that domain of culture in respect of which they are being autonomous.

5. The self-creating person. Autonomous behaviour now becomes reflexive. The person becomes self-determining about the emergence of their self-determination. They consciously take in hand methods of personal and interpersonal development which enhance their capacity for voluntary choice, for becoming more intentional within all domains of experience and action. This means at least three things.

Unravelling. They are at work on restrictions that come from their past, dealing awarely with the limiting effects of childhood trauma and social conditioning. The individual is committed to uncover and dismantle compulsive, and unreflectively conventional, behaviour in every area of living.

Receptivity. They attend carefully to the deliverances of the receptive mind, the background field of everyday consciousness. To become more aware about the exercise of choice and personal power, means also to open more fully to holistic intuition of, and felt participation in, the different realms of being. We need to resonate fully with the background in order to act with relevance in the foreground. External, outgoing action is balanced with attentive passivity. The person will listen as well as speak, be taught as well as teach, notice what is there as well as create what is different.

Relationship. Various forms of association with other persons become paramount, on the principle that personal autonomy only emerges fully in aware relationship with other autonomous persons. It then becomes clear that autonomy is interdependent with two other basic values of social life, co-operation and hierarchy.

This whole process of self-creation, which starts in a largely humanistic mode, dealing with basic issues for the emerging person in this world and in the accessible aspects of the soul, leads over sooner or later into the next category.

6. The self-transfiguring person. Autonomy now reaches out to uncover latent powers within the soul, and to extend ordinary consciousness into realms that were seemingly above it or below it. The person freely chooses, as an extension of their self-determination, to unfold the higher intuitive self, with its access to universal consciousness, and to unseen powers and presences; to plumb the depths of the psyche and so to become grounded in the origins and underlying rhythms of life.

Fired by aspiration and faith, the person uses the seven-fold key to self-transfiguration, working in the heights, in the middle ground, and in the depths, of the soul. The several parts of the key, which I have discussed elsewhere, are: transcendent encounter, the great reversal, invocation, daily action, evocation, grounding, opening to immanence (Heron, 1988).

The cross and circle

Experiential learning is about the emergence of personhood. To use a geometric metaphor and an ancient symbol, the horizontal bar of the compulsive and conventional states is at right angles to the vertical bar of the creative and the self-creative states of personhood. From the point of intersection, the circle of self-transfiguration can expand, as in figure 8.4.

To use a weaving metaphor, the warp of the compulsive and conventional, interlaces the woof of the creative and self-creating dimensions of personhood, forming the fabric of our being, which can be shaped into the garment of self-transfiguration.

To use an organic metaphor, the conventional dimension provides the social ground, the compulsive dimension the loam out of which the plant of the creative person can grow, bearing self-creating leaves and the bloom of self-transfiguration.

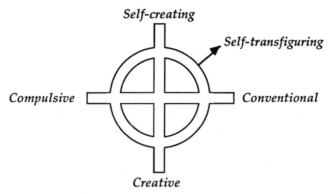

Figure 8.4 *States of personhood*

The valuing dimension: hierarchical mode

By your statements, your proposals, your acts and your presence, you manifest directly to group members your commitment to their fundamental worth as persons. You take strong initiatives in going forth to value people.

1. Culture-setting statements. This overlaps with the same entry under the structuring dimension, hierarchical mode, pages 107-108. Please refer back to this passage.

The special reference here is to statements about the values of the group: that it is a place of safety, support and care, where persons and personhood are fully honoured, cherished and respected.

2. Reaching out. You take initiatives in reaching out to those in the group who are in moments of crisis and affliction, offering your support and skills. You make your care and concern evident in facilitative word and deed.

3. Validation. You appreciate a group member, affirming their intrinsic nature, their qualities, their deeds, to enhance their confidence and self-worth. You affirm the group as a whole for its commitment and growth.

4. Positive feeling. Where appropriate, you directly express your love, affection, liking for a person and how they are being.

5. Holding and touching. Where appropriate, you go forth to hold or touch a person when working or needing support. Your physical presence is nurturing and valuing through contact.

6. Authenticity. You manifest, in direct action, three aspects of authenticity.

1. You are genuine, keeping in touch with your feelings and your own reality: you are there as a person, not alienated, cut off and mechanical within the role.

2. You keep in touch with the real issues in the group, those that engage the group with growth and change.

3. You are immediate, alert to the energy of the group, the spirit that moves through it in surprising and unexpected ways, and you take initiatives to respond to that energy.

7. Active charisma. You actively manifest your presence, your charismatic way of being, as and when appropriate, in and through hierarchical interventions. This is the inward spiritual power of the human person. I have also called this, when training facilitators, distress-free authority. I have written about charismatic training elsewhere (Heron, 1987). Being charismatic and hierarchical in the early stages of training to enable people to be more autonomous and co-operative, is a basic principle of facilitation.

The valuing dimension: co-operative mode

Here you are inclusive, interactive, collaborating with persons in their emergence, in a manner that is founded on respect for their right to self-determination. You are creating a community of value and mutual respect, by eliciting and sharing in this community.

1. Honouring choice. When you invite someone to do some piece of personal development work in the group, you always respect their right to choose to do it or not. So you ask them whether they want to make that choice. If they give you double messages, you hang in with them until they make an unequivocal choice, and then you respect this, whatever it is. If they overtly choose to do the work, then you are truly doing the work with them, not on them or for them. If they choose not to do it, then your honour their right to grow when they want.

2. Co-operation. Working with the group on all the other dimensions, in the co-operative mode, is a basic way of valuing and respecting personhood, and its right to, and need for, self-determination. The art is to know when to move from the hierarchical mode - which provides secrurity for the early embryonic development of self-determination - to the co-operative mode. It can be unwise to rush into the co-operative mode.

3. Mutual affirmation. You collaborate with the group in introducing and setting up a culture in which mutual affirmation occurs. Your prompt and encourage the group to adopt the following:

Nurturing. It becomes an accepted form within the group for members to greet, part, sustain and nourish each other through physical contact.

Validation. In ritual circles and spontaneously at other times, group members learn verbally to express positive feelings - to affirm, appreciate and celebrate each other.

Support. When anyone has personal work to do, members will give that person time, attention, care and support.

4. Mutual authenticity. You collaborate with the group in introducing and sustaining a climate in which each person manifests, in direct action, three aspects of being authentic.

1. Being genuine, keeping in touch with personal feelings and personal reality: being there as a person, not alienated, cut off and mechanical within the role.

2. Keeping in touch with the real *issues* in the group, those that engage it, those at the leading edges of its task and its process.

3. Being immediate, alert to the *energy* of the group, the spirit that moves through it in surprising and unexpected ways, and taking initiatives to respond to that energy.

5. Facilitating participants' charisma. Everyone has the ability to cultivate their personal presence, to manifest their authentic spiritual power. You facilitate the expression of this through charismatic training (Heron, 1987).

The valuing dimension: autonomous mode

You create space for the exercise of individual and group autonomy, the right of persons to be self-determining, their need to be self-creating - in the area of respect for persons, validation and celebration. And simply by being in your presence - as distinct from responding to your acts - people become more self-valuing.

1. Delegation. You can delegate to one member for a time, in the whole group or in sub-groups, the role of facilitating and caring for the group on the valuing dimension. This is followed by feedback to that person.

2. Validation exercise. You set up small groups in which members learn in their own way to affirm and celebrate both themselves and each other.

3. Giving space for autonomy. All the strategies on the other dimensions in the autonomous mode are ways of manifesting respect for persons and their need for self-determination independent of any co-operation and interaction with you. The facilitator who cannot grant this kind of autonomy is acting out their own anxiety about lack of inner freedom and self-determination.

4. Enabling presence. You give abundant free attention to the group: an intense, silent activity of consciousness that encompasses and enhances the autonomy of all those present. Behaviourally it involves the gaze, facial expression, and position relative to others. It is supportive, alert, expectant and invisibly beckoning, waiting for each person in the group to emerge in ways that are meaningful for that person and their fulfilment. It is outside your own distress and anxiety. Its reach is wider and deeper than the manifest behaviour in the group. It is attuned to the potential in each person, to the underlying real issues, to the movements of transforming energy within the group.

5. Going inward. You are centring yourself, finding your own reality, visiting an internal watering place, tapping the inner universe, finding the well-spring of your own emerging person. This is the inner ground for enabling presence.

6. Self-disclosure. This overlaps with being a self-directed client in the structuring dimension, autonomous mode, page 124. You affirm your own autonomy and self-worth, and in this way inspire other members to be the same. You may disclose:

Your beliefs and attitudes about general issues outside the group.

Your thoughts and feelings about your life-experience outside the group.

Your thoughts and feelings about what is going on inside the group at this time, and about the persons concerned.

Your own personal anxieties, conflicts, tensions as these arise within the group process.

Your delights, celebrations, strengths as these arise within the group.

Your own personal growth work as self-directed client, supported by the attention and care of the group.

7. A culture of autonomous authenticity. This is not a strategy. It is a consequence of all the strategies on all the dimensions, especially the valuing dimension. Group members are self-determining in authentic ways of being in the group. I repeat here the range of behaviour from Chapter 2.

Task-oriented. The group is outgoing, busy with the experiential learning cycle, practising some particular skill, undergoing some experience, exploring some issue. Members co-operate in learning, in problem-solving and decision-making.

Process-oriented. The group is ingoing, examining its own psychosocial process, seeking to understand *how* it is functioning.

Expressive. The group is active with celebration and creative expression in word, art, music, song or movement.

Interactive. Group members are engaged in interpersonal work and feedback, giving and receiving impressions, sharing attractions and aversions, withdrawing and owning projections.

Confronting. Members are engaged in creative conflict resolution, in supportive confrontation.

Personal work oriented. Individual members are taking time for personal growth work. Each one has a turn, working in pairs or small groups, or with you in the presence of the whole group. This work covers a wide spectrum, from cognitive and analytic self-discovery, through emotional disclosure, regression and catharsis, to imaginal or ritual transmutation and transpersonal development.

Charismatic. The group is attuning to psychic and spiritual energies, entering altered states of consciousness and action.

9. The creation of a facilitator style

The aim of this chapter is to discuss some of the factors that may contribute to the creation of a facilitative style.

The style is the person

There are some imponderables about a person that constitute their given uniqueness and distinctness of being, and manifest unmistakably in the way they relate to others. This is original or archetypal style, like a person's signature in action. It is not acquired or created. It just becomes more fully revealed as behaviour becomes more and more authentic.

Personal values

Your facilitator style will reflect what you deeply value about human development, what you hold to be really worthwhile forms of human flourishing. For my part, I value *autonomy, co-operation and hierarchy* - and in that order. By autonomy I mean a state of being in which each person can in liberty determine and fulfil their own true needs and interests. By co-operation I mean mutual aid and support between autonomous persons. And by hierarchy I mean a state of being in which someone takes responsibility in doing things to or for other persons for the sake of the future autonomy and co-operation of those persons: this is part of parenthood, education and many professions.

Personal principles

I mean here guiding norms for action that follow from personal values. They are moral principles of high generality. The primary one I use in group work is that of *respect for persons*: each person should be given a free and informed choice about any personal work or group activity, and should be enabled to be autonomous and to co-operate with other such persons.

The purpose and composition of the group

What the group is set up to achieve, its learning objectives, will of course have a strong influence on your facilitator style. So too will the level of skill and relevant experience in group members. Both these factors will affect the way you use the modes of hierarchy, co-operation and autonomy in running the group.

There are many different ways you can combine these modes. Figure 9.1 is a final reminder. At the top are the four elements of a course: learning objectives, course programme, assessment of students, evaluation of the course. Next are the four elements of the course programme: the topics or subject matter, their allocation over time, the human and physical resources available for learning/teaching, and the learning and teaching methods. Then come the seven ways the modes can be combined, giving seven basic kinds of educational polity.

Objectives		Programme		Assessment		Evaluation
Topics		Time		Resources		Methods
	Hierarchy		Co-operation			Autonomy
1.	*You decide all*					
2.	*You decide some*		*You with group decide some*			
3.	*You decide some*		*You with group decide some*			*Group decide some*
4.	*You decide some*					*Group decide some*
5.			*You with group decide some*			*Group decide some*
6.			*You with group decide all*			
7.						*Group decide all*

Figure 9.1 *Anatomy of educational decision-making*

Personal development, training and professional development

The more you, the facilitator, have done personal development work - both in healing the memories through deep regression and catharsis, and in opening up to transpersonal energies and domains - the more flexibility you have within yourself for facilitating these and other processes within your group. Also for moving around freely within the dimensions and modes of facilitation presented in this book.

Working on yourself enables you to keep clear of the pitfalls of the counter-transference, referred to in Chapter 2. If you unawarely project your own hidden distress on to the group, this either contaminates your interventions, making them degenerate rapidly, or it keeps you rigidly contained within a very limited range of interventions.

Good training helps you create your facilitative style, above all by alerting you to a comprehensive range of issues and options, a large repertoire of policies and strategies. It gives you a broad canvas and a wide palette. The purpose of this booklet, as a basis for training, is to stretch your facilitative imagination, to appreciate the great reach and subtlety of the enterprise.

The basic elements of effective training are discrimination, modelling, practice and feedback (Cross, 1976). You need to be able to *discriminate* within a wide repertoire of policies and strategies, to know what's what within it, to be able to pick and choose appropriately from it, to be able to assess your own strengths and weaknesses in relation to this repertoire: which bits of it are you good at, and which not? You need good *modelling*: verbal descriptions or videos or live demonstrations of what it is to make interventions well, in words, in manner and in timing. You need the opportunity to *practise* interventions, especially those you are not good at, in role plays or for real in small groups, and when it goes wrong, to rerun the practice until it goes right. You need *feedback* on your practice from your peers and your trainer, so you can learn how you slip off the track and can get confirmation when you are on it.

Feedback during training needs to be enlarged from time to time to include sessions of self- and peer *assessment*, and of collaborative assessment with your trainer, on your overall performance. This is followed, at the end of training, by a further process of self-, peer and trainer *accreditation*: what you, your peers and your trainer agree in authorizing you to do as a facilitator out there in the community.

Modelling has a further aspect. Many facilitators at the start of their careers have modelled their style on that of some established group leader whom they admire and respect, because they resonate to it. This kind apprenticeship at a distance and by identification has much to recommend it. It gives the beginner a secure platform on which they can eventually evolve and discover their own style.

Professional development continues the learning process during your working career. One valuable form of it is to join a self- and peer supervision group with other facilitators. In such a group each person takes turns sharing critical or problematic incidents from their recent work, receiving comment and feedback from the other group members.

Other forms of professional development include: self-monitoring during your work; self-assessment after your work, using memory, or audio-visual replay; peer assessment from colleagues who work in the same group with you; feedback from members of the group you have led, face to face at the end of a group, or via questionnaires sent in after the group. Assessment and feedback can be on two things: your interventions and style of facilitation; and on the programme and range of activities and methods used. A tool for self-assessment of your facilitator style, using the model of this book, is given at the end of the chapter.

Criteria of excellence

Another way of creating a style is to consider the criteria in the light of which you would judge a facilitator to be competent. There are many overlapping versions of such a set of criteria. Here is one account for the personal and interpersonal development facilitator, which you may like to reflect on - and modify. I state it in terms of you, the facilitator.

1. Authority. You have distress-free authority, and do not displace your own hidden pathology through your interventions.

2. Confrontation. You can confront supportively, and can work effectively on unaware projections and other defensive forms within the group.

3. Orientation. You can provide clear conceptual orientation, as appropriate, in and among the experiential work.

4. Care. You come over to group members as caring, empathic, warm and genuine.

5. Range of methods. You can handle effectively both deep regression and catharsis, and transpersonal work; and you have a wide repertoire of techniques and exercises for personal and interpersonal development.

6. Respect for persons. You can in practice respect fully the autonomy of the person, and the right of participants to choose when to change and grow.

7. Flexibility of style. You can move deftly and flexibly, as every situation needs, between interventions within one dimension, between the different dimensions and between the modes, so that the group dynamic can flourish with growth and learning.

Research

There has been a lot of conventional, old paradigm research on experiential groups - with before and after studies, control groups or comparable groups, the researcher external to the group process. Much of this research has been about the effect of groups on participants, especially after the group is over. But the research method itself is alienated: it does research *on* groups, rather than *with* groups. To do research on people rather than with people is to treat them as less than people. While there have been positive findings using this approach, they are still vitiated by the assumptions of the method.

In the first and 1977 edition of this book, I wrote at considerable length about this issue. Since then, I and others have written a great deal more about the negative case against the old method, and about new paradigm research, which, in the form of co-operative inquiry, does reasearch *with* people. So rather than repeat or revise the earlier text, I refer the reader to the relevant literature since 1981 (Reason and Rowan, 1981; Heron and Reason, 1981, 1982; Heron, 1984; Heron and Reason, 1985; Reason, 1988).

Co-operative inquiry breaks down the distinction between researcher and subject, and moves between the poles of reflection and action. The initiating researcher co-opts the group members as coresearchers who contribute to the thinking that generates, designs, manages and reviews the research; he or she also joins them as cosubjects, who undertake the actions and experiences that are being researched.

Experiential learning groups, when they use the experiential learning cycle, as depicted in Chapter 4 and again in Chapter 7, are already busy with an incipient form of co-operative inquiry. It lends itself readily to transformation into full-blown forms of person-centred research.

What does research contribute to the way in which you create a facilitator style? Conventional, old-style research on trainer effectiveness has, within its severe limits, affirmed the value of 2, 3 and 4 in the list in the previous section on criteria of facilitator excellence (Bolman, 1976).

More to the point, the new paradigm of co-operative inquiry can inspire a whole *way* of facilitating groups, by elevating learning to participative research, moving between the poles of reflection and experience. And the references cited a few paragraphs above include many accounts of co-operative inquiries in specific fields, from which specialist facilitators can cull findings to enhance their style and practice.

It is, however, important to remember that research with persons does not tell you, *through its findings,* what is really worthwhile or what you ought to do, for these things are a matter of moral vision, not of empirical inquiry. But collective reflection within the ambience of a co-operative inquiry may enhance insight into basic ethical values and principles. And the outcomes of the inquiry may show what is involved in the effective (and ineffective) realization of that insight.

Social change

How does a commitment to social and politcal change affect and shape your facilitator style? It can certainly determine what sort of workshops you run as defined in terms of their main objectives.

1. Personal *and* cultural/planetary issues. You may want to run workshops that always deal with existential and archaic anxiety in the context of cultural/ planetary anxiety (see Chapter 2 for these three sorts of anxiety). Personal distress is seen as bound up with cultural oppression and lack of global awareness. My belief is that personal and interpersonal development will increasingly be seen as interdependent with planetary commitment, by which I mean a concern with fostering the well-being of all life forms and their habitat, locally, nationally and globally.

2. Transfer to life-style and life-planning. You may want to include in your workshops time for members to commit themselves to revisions of their life-style and life-plan, or you may choose to let this process happen by spontaneous transfer, after the workshop.

3. Professional, organizational and community development. You may be committed to change the existing social system from within, by working for new attitudes, skills and methods within existing professions, organizations and community associations.

4. Soft revolution and non-violent training. You may want to confront more directly the rigidities of the existing social system, by training people in creative subversion of oppressive institutions, or non-violent interruption of their activities.

5. Alternative network training. You may want to train and set up peer self-help networks that constitute an alternative to existing institutional and professional services. There are self-help mutual aid groups for those in life-crisis, or with special physical or social disabilities, or oppressed by prejudice and discrimination, or with special revisionary and reforming interests; and of course for personal and social development and awareness - as in co-counselling networks.

6. Alternative institutions. You may want a workshop to prepare for the setting up of alternative kinds of institution: in industry, commerce, medicine, education, the family, community, and so on.

Making a self-assessment profile of your facilitator style

Set up an 18-part grid with the six dimensions across the top, and the three modes down the sides; then divide each of the 18 boxes into an upper and a lower half, as shown in figure 9.2.

Take just one kind of group that you run - your assessment might be different for different kinds of groups. First estimate quantity only: that is, how much you work in each of the 18 parts, regardless of the quality of that work. Enter 3 in the lower left of the box if you work a lot, 2 for a medium amount, 1 for only a little, and 0 for not at all. Remember that 'how much you work' means not only how much you actively *do*, but how much *time* you give to a mode. This applies particularly to the autonomous mode: if you arrange for the group to have a lot of autonomous learning on a dimension, this merits a high score, even though you may not be doing much while your group is busy with it.

	Planning	Meaning	Confronting	Feeling	Structuring	Valuing
Hierarchy						
Co-operation						
Autonomy						

Figure 9.2 *Form for self-assessment*

The maximum for each vertical column added up is 6. So if on any one dimension you work an equal amount in the hierarchical, co-operative and autonomous modes, you put not more than 2 in each of the respective boxes. Of course, if you don't work a lot in that dimension as a whole, then you would only put 1 in each of the mode boxes. There is no minimum score for each vertical column sum, it could be anything down to and including 0.

The totals of each of these vertical columns side by side reveal how much or how little you work in each of the six dimensions as a whole. If these figures don't seem to be quite correct in representing the different dimensions, change them until they feel right, then work back into the grid, adjusting the figures for the modes. If you take a total for each of the horizontal lines, then you will get a weighting for how much you work, overall, in the different modes.

Then assess the quality of your work in each box. Enter a second figure in the lower right part of each box, after the quantity figure: put 3 if you judge your work to be of high quality, 2 for medium quality, 1 for low quality, and 0 for dismal and degenerate quality. If the quantity figure is 0, again put 3, 2, 1, or 0 beside it, but these now mean that the absence of any work in that area is, respectively, a good thing, a not so good thing, a poor thing, or a very bad thing. Now you have a double entry in the lower half of each of the 18 boxes. Thus 32 means you do a lot of work of medium quality, 13 means a small amount of high quality, and so on. If you get perplexed about what good quality is, brood on the criteria of excellence given earlier in this chapter.

Now assess whether you need to change the quantity of work you do in each part. This means two things: doing more or less on each of the six dimensions; and within each dimension, doing more or less in each of the three modes. Reflect on the dimensions, then work back into the modes.

Then put a figure in the top left of each of the 18 parts. It may be more or less than, or the same as, the figure below it - which is the figure for existing quantity - depending on whether you want to increase or reduce the amount or keep it the same.

Finally, in the upper right of the box put a small arrow pointing upwards, if the figure in the lower right is 2, two small upward arrows if the figure below is 1, and three if it is 0, and put a tick if it is 3. This is just to indicate the degree to which quality needs to improve, if you have judged it be less than 3, that is, high.

You now have a comprehensive profile of your facilitator style for a given kind of group. The profile indicates both what your style is like now, and what you would like it to become in the future. Experiment with other ways of making visual analogues of your profile.

Making this profile is a subtle and demanding exercise. It presupposes that you have a good grasp of the set of options represented by each of the 18 parts of the grid. It is best to do the assessment thinking out loud with a colleague, starting with an overall sense of where you are on the dimensions and modes, then refining it down into figures on the 18-part grid. Your colleague can assist, prompt, pace and confront your emerging self-assessment. Then you reverse roles. At the end of being in both roles, you will have greatly extended your imaginative grasp of facilitator style and options, both in general, and in relation to your own profile.

References

Bolman, L. 'Group Leader Effectiveness', in Cooper, C. (Ed), *Developing Social Skills in Managers*, Macmillan, London, 1976.

Boud, D. (Ed), *Developing Student Autonomy in Learning*, Kogan Page, London, 1988.

Cross, K. P. *Accent on Learning*, Jossey Bass, London, 1976.

Harrison, R. 'Developing Autonomy, Initiative and Risk-taking through a Laboratory Design', *European Training*, Vol. 2, pp. 100-117, 1973.

Heron, J. *Dimensions of Facilitator Style*, first edition, Human Potential Resource Group, University of Surrey, 1977.

Heron, J. 'Self and Peer Assessment', in Boydell, T. and Pedlar, M. (Eds), *Handbook of Management Self-Development*, Gower, London, 1981.

Heron, J. and Reason, P. *Co-counselling: An Experiential Inquiry I* (1981) and *II* (1982), Human Potential Resource Group, University of Surrey, 1981, 1982.

Heron, J. *Education of the Affect*, Human Potential Resource Group, University of Surrey, 1983.

Heron, J. *Co-operative Inquiry into Altered States of Consciousness*, Human Potential Resource Group, University of Surrey, 1984, revised in Reason (1988).

Heron, J. and Reason, P. *Whole Person Medicine: A Cooperative Inquiry*, British Postgraduate Medical Federation, University of London, 1985.

Heron, J. *Six Category Intervention Analysis*, third edition, Human Potential Resource Group, University of Surrey, 1989, first edition, 1975.

Heron, J. *Confessions of a Janus-Brain*, Endymion Press, London, 1987.

Heron, J. *Cosmic Psychology*, Endymion Press, London, 1988.

Heron, J. 'Assessment Revisited', in Doud, D. (Ed), *Developing Student Autonomy in Learning*, Kogan Page, London, 1988a.

Heron, J. 'Validity in Co-operative Inquiry', in Reason, P. (Ed), *Human Inquiry in Action*, Sage, London, 1988b.

Hillman, J. *Revisioning Psychology*, Harper and Row, New York, 1975.

Jung, C. G. *Man and his Symbols*, W. H. Allen, London, 1964.

Knowles, M. S. *The Modern Practice of Adult Education: From Pedagogy to Andragogy*, Follett, Chicago, 1980.

Reason, P. and Rowan, J. (Eds), *Human Inquiry: A Sourcebook of New Paradigm Research*, Wiley, Chichester, 1981.

Reason, P. (Ed), *Human Inquiry in Action*, Sage, London, 1988.

Index